AN EXPLANATION

OF

THE CONSTITUTION

OF THE

UNITED STATES OF AMERICA.

PREPARED FOR USE IN CATHOLIC SCHOOLS,
ACADEMIES, AND COLLEGES.

———

BY

FRANCIS T. FUREY, A.M.

———

With a new introduction by
John R. Vile
Middle Tennessee State University,
Murfreesboro, TN

THE LAWBOOK EXCHANGE, LTD.
Clark, New Jersey

ISBN 978-1-61619-506-9

Lawbook Exchange edition 2015

The quality of this reprint is equivalent to the quality of the original work.

THE LAWBOOK EXCHANGE, LTD.
33 Terminal Avenue
Clark, New Jersey 07066-1321

*Please see our website for a selection of our other publications
and fine facsimile reprints of classic works of legal history:*
www.lawbookexchange.com

Library of Congress Cataloging-in-Publication Data

Furey, Francis T. (Francis Thomas), 1852- author.
  An explanation of the constitution of the United States of America :
prepared for use in Catholic schools, academies, and colleges / by Francis T.
Furey; with a new introduction by John R. Vile, Middle Tennessee State
University, Murfreesboro, TN. -- Lawbook Exchange ed. 2015.
     pages cm
  Includes introduction: A constitutional catechism from a Roman Catholic
perspective.
  Includes bibliographical references.
  ISBN 978-1-61619-506-9 (hardcover : alk. paper)
  1. Constitutional law--United States--Miscellanea. 2. United States--
Politics and government--Miscellanea. 3. Catholics--United States--
Handbooks, manuals, etc. 4. Furey, Francis T. (Francis Thomas), 1852-.
An explanation of the constitution of the United States of America. I.
Vile, John R., writer of introduction. II. Title.
  KF4550.Z9.F867 2015
  342.7302--dc23
                                    2014047466

Printed in the United States of America on acid-free paper

INTRODUCTION

A CONSTITUTIONAL CATECHISM FROM A ROMAN CATHOLIC PERSPECTIVE

In an introduction to an *Elementary Catechism on the Constitution of the United States*, which Arthur J. Stansbury, a Presbyterian minister, first published in 1831, I noted that it was logical to use the catechistic mechanism, which had long been used to teach the tenets of religion, to teach the U.S. Constitution.[1] I further cited a number of other constitutional catechisms including John Rose's catechism of the British Constitution, which he published in 1795[2], and catechisms on the U.S. Constitution by John S. Hart in 1871,[3] by Lewis Cruger in 1863,[4] and by John Wilford Overall in 1896,[5] and other volumes, including one of my own, which I have since updated,[6] which employed a question-and-answer format typical of a catechism

---

[1] John R. Vile, "Of Catechisms, Religious and Constitutional," Introduction of Arthur J. Stansbury, *Elementary Catechism on the Constitution of the United States for the Use of Schools* (Clark, NJ: The Lawbook Exchange, 2013), pp. v–xx.
[2] *A Constitution Catechism Adapted to all Ranks and Capacities, Illustrated with . . . Notes: Principally Extracted from the Commentaries of . . . Judge Blackstone. To which is Prefixed an Epistolary Dedication to . . . Thomas Erskine* (Bristol: Printed and sold by the author, 1795).
[3] *A Brief Exposition of the Constitution of the United States for the Use of Common Schools* (Philadelphia: E.H. Butler & Co., 1871).
[4] Cruger, *Catechism of the Constitution of the United States: A Brief Exposition of the True Elementary Principles of that Great Compact Between Sovereign States* (n.p.: 1863).
[5] Overall, *A Catechism of the Constitution of the United States of America. With Sketches of the Constitutional and Ratifying Conventions; and Valuable Personal, Historical, Political and Legal Information, Criticism and Interpretation Adapted to Students and Statesmen* (New York: The Author, 1896 [1905]).
[6] John R. Vile, *The United States Constitution: Questions and Answers*, 2nd ed (Santa Barbara, CA, ABC-CLIO, 2014).

without using this term in its title. [7] At the time, I was unaware of Francis T. [Thomas] Furey's volume on the U.S. Constitution reprinted here, *An Explanation of the Constitution of the United States of America* (1889) which follows a catechism format.[8] Having since discovered it, I believe that this book can lend important insight not only to the genre but that it can also contribute to an understanding of the role of Catholic education in the United States, and to more recent increases in the number of Protestant schools and homeschoolers in America.

Publication and Audience

Furey's book follows the Stansbury volume by more than 50 years, and it is almost twice the length, perhaps largely because it is aimed for an older audience of students "in Catholic schools, academies and colleges."[9] More interestingly, while Stansbury's volume appears to have been a stand-alone text, Furey's volume is clearly part of a developing genre of books designed specifically for Roman Catholic educational institutions. The back cover of Furey's book lists 10 Catholic readers, including one for "young ladies," which appear to mimic the organization of the highly moralistic McGuffey Readers that were so widely used in public schools.[10] Incidentally, all these primers were authored by the Rev. J.L. Spalding, D.D., who is identified as the Bishop of Peoria. Similarly, the books describe on the back cover include two spellers, several histories (under which Furey's

---

[7] See, for example Sol Bloom, "Questions and Answers Pertaining to the Constitution," *The Story of the Constitution* (Washington, D.C.: United States Constitutional Sesquicentennial Commission, 1937), pp. 162–178;

[8] Furey, *An Explanation of the Constitution of the United States of America. Prepared for Use in Catholic Schools, Academies, and Colleges* (New York: The Catholic Publication Society Co., 1889).

[9] Taken from the title.

[10] The books were among the most widely published in the nineteenth century. See Etta B. Degering, *McGuffey: The Greatest Forgotten Man* (Hagerstown, MD: Autumn House Publishing, 2011); Quentin R. Skrabec, Jr., *William McGuffey: Mentor to American Industry* (Algora Publishing, 2009); and John H. Westerhoff, *McGuffey and His Readers: Piety, Morality, and Education in Nineteenth-Century America*. Mott Media: 1982.

volume is listed), a book on arithmetic, five religious catechisms, two composition and rhetoric books, a book on astronomy, and a series of copy-books, all by The Catholic Publication Society Co., listed at 9 Barclay Street, New York, N.Y. and managed by Lawrence Kehoe. The back cover further notes that "Other schools books are also in preparation" and that sample copies are available for one-fourth of the unspecified retail price.[11]

If one knew little other than the back cover, it would be clear that by 1889, Roman Catholics had a fairly extensive set of books for their schools. The variety would further suggest that there was a fairly extensive market for such texts. Similarly, one indication of the rise of the modern home-school movement is the fact that there are a number of publishers who cater specifically to this audience.[12]

Francis T. Furey

The back cover identifies Furey only by his A.M. degree. He would later author *a Life of Leo XIII and History of His Pontificate (from official and approved sources),*[13] and a *New and Complete History of the World.*[14] An advertisement in a magazine in 1907 would further list him as a Professor in History and Literature and as one of five editors of an 8-volume *Universal Self-Pronouncing Encyclopedia.*[15] He also translated a number of books. Like many nineteenth-century immigrants, Furey was born in Ireland (Donegal) in 1852. He was educated in Ireland, in Paris, at St. Johns College at Fordham University, and apparently spent most of his life in Philadelphia where, in addition to editing, he taught Latin and history at a local high

[11] The back cover of John S. Hart, *A Brief Exposition of the Constitution of the United States for the Use of Common Schools* (Philadelphia: E.H. Butler & Co., 1871), has a similarly long list of "Approved School Books" that span multiple subjects.
[12] A search of the internet reveals that these range all the way from Bob Jones University Press to Houghton Mifflin Harcourt.
[13] Published by the Catholic Education Society in 1903.
[14] Illinois: A. B. Kuhlman Company, 1906.
[15] *The Business Philosopher*, Vol. 3, Part 2, July, 1907.

school from 1904 to 1907.[16] In 1887, the centennial year of the U.S. Constitution, Furey served as the Recording Secretary of the American Catholic Historical Society of Philadelphia.

The Rise of Catholic Education in America

Although they were a growing presence, fed by immigration from Ireland, Germany, and southern Europe, Roman Catholics were a clear minority in the United States in 1889. Early American education is often associated with New England. The famous "Old Deluder Satan Act"[17] of Puritan Massachusetts specifically mandated that each township build and maintain its own school house largely to train individuals so that they could read the Bible. At the time, there was little thought of separating secular from religious education.

As the Enlightenment and the U.S. Constitution spread ideas of separating church and state, most religious schools were transformed into free public schools. In 1852, Massachusetts adopted a law requiring the attendance of all children between the ages of eight and fourteen.[18] Horace Mann, the first secretary of the Massachusetts Board of Education, is usually identified as the father of this movement, which eventually spread throughout the nation.[19] Neil G. McCluskey observed that Mann aimed for "nonsectarian" Christianity, which "was basically [John] Locke's Christian deism with a thick overlay of phrenology. Christianity for Mann was the Christianity of the Ten Commandments, the Golden Rule, the Beatitudes, the example of Christ."[20] Such

---

[16] *Who Was Who in America, 70th Anniversary, 1898–1968 edition*, vol. IV, 1961–1968 (Chicago, IL: Marqueis-Who's Who., Inc., 1968).

[17] The name came from the law's statement that one of the chief objects "of that old deluder, Satan" was "to keep men from the knowledge of the scriptures." Quoted in David Carleton, *Landmark Congressional Laws on Education* (Westport, CT: Greenwood Press, 2002), p. 2.

[18] Harold A. Buetow, *Of Singular Benefit: The Story of Catholic Education in the United States* (New York: The Macmillan Company, 1970), p. 110.

[19] See Jonathan Messerli, *Horace Mann: A Biography* (New York: Knopf, 1972) and Bob Pepperman Taylor, *Horace Mann's Troubling Legacy: The Education of Democratic Citizens* (Lawrence: University Press of Kansas, 2010).

[20] *Catholic Viewpoints on Education* (Garden City, NY: Hanover House, 1959), p. 23.

teaching was often tied to efforts to proselytize and Americanize Catholic immigrants. One Presbyterian minister was quoted as saying "that the Bible and Common Schools were two stones of the mill that would grind Catholicity out of Catholics."[21]

Although the schools were secular in name, they tended to embody a generic Protestantism, which often included reading the King James Version (KJV) of the Bible in classes. In a case arising in the police court in Boston in 1859, a court upheld a teacher's authority to hit a student on his palms with a thick rattan stick for thirty minutes until he transgressed instructions from his priest and repeated the Lord's Prayer and the Ten Commandments from the KJV.[22] In such circumstances, Roman Catholics altered between thinking that the schools were irreligious and identifying them as pro-Protestant.

The school question was the subject of a number of Provincial Councils that the Catholic Church held in Baltimore beginning in 1829, when bishops began advocating distinctively Catholic schools and texts.[23] In 1890, at a convention of the National Education Association meeting in St. Paul, Minnesota, Cardinal John Ireland of St. Paul responded to accusations that Catholics wanted to abolish public schools by acknowledging the need for free public schools while also defending the parish schools that were by then educating more than 750,000 students.[24] He nonetheless argued that "The state school tends to eliminate religion from the minds and hearts of the youth of the country."[25] He further charged that by occupying students' lives for so much of the day, the public school "crowds out the Church."[26] Much like many modern proponents of home schools or Christian education (who have often been motivated by concerns about "Evolution, sex education, and the somewhat-

---

[21] McCluskey, *Catholic Viewpoints on Education*, p. 29.
[22] *Commonwealth v. Cooke*, 7 Am L. Reg. 417. Explained in *The Encyclopedia of the First Amendment*, ed. By John R. Vile, David L. Hudson, Jr., and David Schultz, 2 vols (Washington, D.C.: CQ Press, 2009), I, 316–317.
[23] McCleskey, *Catholic Viewpoints on Education*, p. 31.
[24] John Ireland, "State Schools and Parish Schools," in Neil G. McCluskey, *Catholic Education in America: A Documentary History* (New York: Teachers College, Columbia University, 1964), pp. 127–140.
[25] *Ibid.*, p. 131.
[26] *Ibid.*, p. 133.

vague but alarming notion of 'secular humanism '"[27] or simply by concerns that public schools were mediocre), Ireland said that the public schools offered a religion of "secularism."[28] This argument was in some tension with his argument that public schools embodied a generic Protestantism:

> Well-meaning men propose as a remedy to teach a common Christianity in the schools. This will not do. In loyalty to their principles, Catholics cannot and will not accept a common Christianity. To Catholics, what does not bear on its face the stamp of Catholicity is Protestant in form and in implication, even if it be Catholic in substance."[29]

Ireland further advocated a controversial plan whereby Catholics would rent their schools to public authorities but teach religion after school hours (just as Protestants could engage in religious exercises outside of school times).[30] In a follow-up speech, he clarified that although he thought that "factional Christianity [Protestantism] is better than materialism,"[31] Catholics should be equally entitled to have their tax monies go to Catholic schools as Protestants were entitled to have theirs go to public schools.

Although they rarely succeeded in persuading governments to use state funds for Catholic education,[32] in time many Catholic parishes thought that it was essential to the perpetuation of their faith to create their own schools, and the U.S. Supreme Court eventually recognized the right of parents to educate their children in such schools in its landmark decision in *Pierce v.*

---

[27] Milton Gaither, "Why Homeschooling Happened," *Educational Horizons* 86 (Summer 2008): pp. 226–237. Also see Gaither's *Homeschool: An American History* (New York: Palgrave Macmillan, 2008).

[28] *Ibid.*, p. 131.

[29] *Ibid.*, p. 135.

[30] *Ibid.*, p. 139.

[31] *Ibid.*, p. 147.

[32] In 1875, Representative James G. Blaine introduced a constitutional amendment to prohibit any states from spending money for schools "under the control of any religious sect or denomination" or to divide moneys among them. Although it was never adopted, many states passed their own Blaine Amendments. See "Blaine Amendment," John R. Vile, *Encyclopedia of Constitutional Amendments, Proposed Amendments, and Amending Issues, 1789–2010* (Santa Barbara, CA: ABC-CLIO, 2010), I, 49–50.

Society of Sisters (1925).[33] In this respect, Catholics shared many sentiments with modern fundamentalists who find their own faiths at war with what they believe to be the secular religion of the classroom.

Although Catholics considered themselves to be distinctive, they also regarded themselves as patriotic. Many were troubled by nativist (anti-immigrant) and anti-Catholic sentiments that they found in public school texts, many of which associated republicanism with opposition to any priests or hierarchies, including that of the Catholic Church. It is difficult to know whether they were more threatened by texts that specifically denigrated their religion or by those that ignored religion altogether.

Furey's General Critique of Civic Education

These concerns were not simply spiritual. Furey's Preface is extremely enlightening in this regard. Almost as though he were advocating contemporary common core standards (or objecting that they were too lax), he observed that many believe that education in his day was too much directed to covering too many subjects without training students in "the art of learning."[34] Like modern advocates of civic education, Furey further commented on how some schools altogether omitted teaching about government or treat it "only in the most careless and superficial manner."[35]

Furey's preface was a window into the approach that his book would take. Like other expositors of the Constitution, he would praise the Document, but he would assert (he provided no details) that the Constitution was not only compatible with, but also similar to, Catholicism:

---

[33] 268 U.S. 510. Two years earlier, in *Meyer v. Nebraska*, 262 U.S. 390, the Court had upheld the right of schools to teach foreign languages, a practice often associated with religious schools (in this case Lutheran) that thought it important to teach the language (German) of national origin.

[34] Furey, p. 5.

[35] *Ibid.*, pp. 5–6. Hart had voiced a similar concern in his *Brief Exposition of the Constitution* in 1871, pp. 3–4.

for there is no other [framework of government] in the world
that in its constitution and character so closely resembles that
of the Catholic Church as does the United States Government;
there is no county in which the Church enjoys more freedom
than she does in ours, and there is none in which she is more
prosperous. Nor has the United States any class of citizens that
are more loyal to her institutions than are the Catholics.[36]

Furey further portrayed his text as one that would further imbue
such loyalty by conveying accurate information. In describing
Stansbury's book, I observed that he rarely mentioned Supreme
Court decisions; Furey's book follows a similar course, perhaps
demonstrating that the idea of largely interpreting the document
through such decisions is largely a twentieth and twenty-first
century phenomenon.

Furey divided his book into 44 chapters, each, consistent
with a catechism, that consisted of a series of questions and
answers. The first four chapters largely deal with historical
materials, including types of governments, and the experience
under the Articles of Confederation, while chapters four through
38 follow the outline of the U.S. Constitution, chapters 39
through 42 deal with subsequent amendments, and the remaining
two chapters deal with state and city governments, the latter of
which receive no direct attention in the U.S. Constitution. By
comparison to modern volumes, Furey's provided relatively little
information on the Bill of Rights, but it is important to remember
that he was writing at a time before the U.S. Supreme Court had
decided that the due process clause of the Fourteenth
Amendment applied most of these limitations not only to the
national government but also to the states.[37]

Furey's work rarely departed from constitutional orthodoxy
and has minimal mistakes. One arguable weakness is that he
devoted relatively little attention to the Constitutional
Convention of 1787 and inaccurately referred to its "unpre-

---

[36] *Ibid.*, p. 6.
[37] Henry J. Abraham and Barbara A. Perry, *Freedom and the Court: Civil
Rights & Liberties in the United States*, 8th ed. (Lawrence: University Press of
Kansas, 2003), pp. 33–105.

cedented unanimity."[38] He gave more credit to Lincoln's Emancipation Proclamation than to the Thirteenth Amendment for the abolition of slavery.[39] On the whole, however, the work is less notable for its eccentricities than for its distinctively Catholic perspective.

Even though Furey designed his questions and answers for both high school and college students, they are fairly straightforward. Furey did not so much design them to elicit independent thinking about what students thought the Constitution should mean or to examine rival theories of constitutional interpretation but to encourage mastery of a set of distinct facts about the Constitution. In this respect, Furey further demonstrated the affinity of his book with earlier catechisms, both religious and constitutional.

Issues Related to Catholicism

While many nineteenth-century Protestants might seek to contrast the democratic/republican government of the United States with the rule of a foreign pontiff, Furey saw no conflict. Not only did he claim that no other constitution "so closely resembles that of the Catholic Church as does the United States Government," but in discussing other forms of government, the examples that he provided of theocracies, or "Government of a state by the immediate direction of God," were "the ancient Jewish state. . . . the Puritan commonwealth of New England and the Mormon organization of Utah Territory."[40] Furey further said that "free and popular government" is "best secured" through "the English parliamentary, or representative, system as modified and applied in the United States."[41]

Somewhat later, Furey observed that Catholics "should take a special interest in this Constitution" because "in its form it approaches nearer to the Canon Law than any other such secular

---

[38] *Ibid.*, p. 29.
[39] *Ibid.*, p. 79.
[40] *Ibid.*, p. 10.
[41] *Ibid.*, p. 11.

instrument."[42] A notice of "New Publications" in a prominent Catholic magazine futher observed that "in no other country in the world have the principles of civil government so intimate a harmony with those of our holy religion, it is the home of intelligence and liberty that the fairest fruit of personal sanctification can thrive."[43] Furey further observed that Catholics have accepted the document "with the fullest gratitude towards the fathers of the country who framed it" and that its signers included Catholics Thomas FitzSimons of Pennsylvania, and Daniel Carroll of Maryland, who are described as "two of the most prudent, conservative, and patriotic of them all."[44]

Religious Tolerance

Furey acknowledged that the "prevailing religion" at the time the Constitution was written was "Protestantism of various forms," but he also noted that Catholics were also present, most notably in Maryland and Pennsylvania."[45] In a strategy that imitated other Catholic textbooks of the era,[46] he observed that Catholics, including Columbus, had originally discovered and explored the continent.[47] Moreover, the English claim had been established "In 1496, by Cabot, a Venetian and a Catholic, in the Service of the Catholic King Henry VII."[48]

Whereas Protestants might identify Catholicism with religious intolerance, Furey turned the tables. Not incorrectly, he identified the early religious policy of most of the colonies as that of "intolerance towards all denominations but the ruling sect," but noted that Maryland, which had been settled by Catholics,

---

[42] *Ibid.*, p. 29.
[43] *Catholic World*, Vol. 50 (1889), p. 281. No author listed.
[44] *Ibid.*
[45] *Ibid.*, p. 17.
[46] Joseph Moreau, "Rise of the (Catholic) American Nation: United States History and Parochial Schools, 1878–1925," *American Studies* 38 (Fall, 1997), pp. 67–90.
[47] Furey, p. 17.
[48] *Ibid.*, p. 19. Henry VII, of course, preceded the founding of the English (Anglican) Church.

practiced "general toleration and equality for all Christians."[49] He further associated the First Continental Congress with "a more ample Bill of Rights"[50] and the Declaration of Independence with the nation's "baptism," while acknowledging that some of the colonists' disgust with Britain stemmed from "The Quebec Act, granting full religious and political liberty to the Catholics of Canada,"[51] and was thus at least party "anti-Catholic." He proudly noted that there were "only a few" Catholic Tories (American supporters of Britain), that George Meade, A Catholic in Philadelphia, had signed the non-importation resolutions of 1765, that Charles Carroll of Carrollton, signed the Declaration of Independence and "put more wealth at stake than all the other signers together," and that he and his cousin, Rev. John Carroll (a future bishop and archbishop of Baltimore) had sought to enlist Canadian help.[52] Somewhat later in the book Furey indicated that Charles Carroll also once owned the land on which the nation's capital would later stand.[53] Still further on he observed that Cardinal Gibbons had "pronounced the closing prayer" at the centenary celebration of the adoption of the Constitution that had been celebrated in Philadelphia in 1887.[54]

Slavery and Native Americans

Two issues that mar America's founding are slavery and its treatment of Native Americans. In referring to the Department of the Interior, Furey observed that Catholics had sometimes found fault with it because "of gross injustice done to Catholic missionaries among the Indians, and to Indian tribes converted to Catholicity."[55] Similarly, he said that Catholics should rejoice over the Emancipation Proclamation and the Thirteenth Amendment because "the Church has ever striven in the same

---

[49] Furey, p. 21.
[50] Ibid., p. 24.
[51] Ibid. Furey would refer to this act again on p. 136.
[52] Ibid., 26.
[53] Ibid., p.. 76.
[54] Ibid., p. 39.
[55] Ibid., p. 89.

direction, either doing away with slavery altogether where she could, or trying to mitigate its severities where she could not abolish it."[56] One might see some disconnect between this stance and Furey's identification of Chief Justice Roger Taney as "the most eminent Catholic civilian of this country," but Furey chose to focus on Taney's position rather than on his unmentioned decision declaring that Blacks were not and could not be U.S. citizens in the Dred Scott case.[57]

Test Oaths

Furey discussed religion and the Constitution when discussing test oaths and the First Amendment. In describing the prohibition of test oaths as "a remarkable provision," Furey observed that such oaths had previously been used to exclude Catholics from office.[58] He further observed that with the oaths lifted, "Catholics have held almost every office, except those of President and Vice-President, from the Chief Justiceship of the Supreme Court down."[59] Little could he know that no Catholic would occupy the presidential office until the election of John F. Kennedy in 1960.

First Amendment

In what appears to be a reference to the establishment clause, which originally prohibited federal interference with existing state establishments of religion, Furey traced the development of religious liberty in the First Amendment to "religious intolerance," explaining that New Hampshire "did not want its religious condition at that time to be interfered with."[60] He further identified New Hampshire as the "most intolerant" state in the Union because it continued to bar Catholics from state

---

[56] *Ibid.*, p. 144.
[57] *Ibid.*, p. 113. 19 How. (60 U.S.). 393 (1857).
[58] *Ibid.*, p. 133.
[59] *Ibid.*, p. 133.
[60] *Ibid.*, p. 135.

offices.[61] In one of his few generic references to Supreme Court decisions, Furey restrictively interpreted the First Amendment to "prohibit the free exercise of any form of Christianity" explaining that "it has been decided by the Supreme Court that Christianity is a fundamental part of our Constitution."[62]

This may have been a further attempt to reconcile his writings with Pope Leo XVIII's 1885 condemnation of what he considered to be excessive American individualism and any attempts to separate church and state.[63] Furey's overview view is much more consistent with the praise of such separation that John Courtney Murray and other American Catholic philosophers would later articulate.[64]

Perhaps because the book was designed for upper grades and college classes, Furey resorted to little outright moral instruction in his book. In discussing the compensation of the president, he did mention "worldly gain" perhaps implying that there were potential spiritual rewards as well.[65] Similarly, in writing about bankruptcy, he said that if a debtor "afterwards acquires the means, he is bound in conscience to pay as much of his former obligations as he can,"[66] and in describing judges, he mentioned the need for "upright men"[67] but the book is otherwise free of the

---

[61] *Ibid.*, pp. 135–136.

[62] *Ibid.*, p. 136. Furey is probably referring to the decision in *Church of the Holy Trinity v. United States*, 143 U.S. 457 (1892), in which Justice David J. Brewer described the United States as a "Christian nation." See *Encyclopedia of the First Amendment*, , I, 174–275.

[63] *Immortale Dei*, http://www.vatican.va/holy_father/leo?xiii/encyclicals/documents/hf?--xiii_enc_0111188. Thus, in paragraph 7, Leo observed that it "is a sin for the State not to have care for religion as a something beyond its scope, or as of no practical benefit; or out of many forms of religion to adopt that one which chimes in with the fancy; for we are bound absolutely to worship God in that way which He has shown to be His will. All who rule, therefore, would hold in honour the holy name of God, and one of their chief duties must be to favour religion, to protect it, to shield it under the credit and sanction of the laws, and neither to organize nor enact any measure that may compromise its safety."

[64] See Murray, *Religious Liberty: Catholic Struggles with Pluralism* (Westminster: John Knox Press, 1993) and Murray, *We Hold These Truths: Catholic Reflections on the American Prospect* (Sheed & Ward, 2005).

[65] Furey, p. 100.

[66] *Ibid.*, p. 68.

[67] Furey, p. 105.

kind of moralizing instruction that is found in other texts of the period, including the previously-mentioned McGuffey Readers.

Conclusion

Over the last century, many Protestants have followed the Roman Catholic model in setting up their own schools—including colleges like Liberty University, which was founded by pastor Jerry Fallwell and has been a leader in distance education, and Patrick Henry College, which was founded by Michael Farris, who also founded the Home School Legal Defense Association (HSLDA)—where they seek to preserve Christian values. In addition to those who are enrolled in Christian schools, it has been estimated that the number of homeschooled students currently ranges "from 1.1 to 2 million."[68] As indicated earlier, many of these students use materials specifically written for them. Some materials suggest that the U.S. is a Christian nation; others put great emphasis on how the First Amendment protects the rights to free exercise.

Furey's volume provides a window on similar teachings by Roman Catholics in the nineteenth century. It is a worthy supplement to earlier catechisms and readers in the public schools. Much as a text in an individual state would have sought to glorify the achievements of its citizens, Furey put special emphasis on the achievements of Roman Catholics. Although Furey conveyed relatively little theological content, he sought to convey a sense of pride in Catholic readers and the message that being a good Catholic was consistent with being a good and informed citizen. This is similar to the themes of texts used by modern parents and teachers who continue to believe that religious or home schooling contributes to moral development and best conveys the history and values of their proponents.

John R. Vile

---

[68] Kimberly A. Yuracko, "Education Off the Grid: Constitutional Constraints on Homeschooling," *California Law Review* 96 (February, 2008), p. 124.

AN EXPLANATION

OF

THE CONSTITUTION

OF THE

UNITED STATES OF AMERICA.

PREPARED FOR USE IN CATHOLIC SCHOOLS,
ACADEMIES, AND COLLEGES.

BY

FRANCIS T. FUREY, A.M.

NEW YORK:
THE CATHOLIC PUBLICATION SOCIETY CO.,
9 BARCLAY STREET.

1889.

CONTENTS.

4   *CONTENTS.*

PREFACE.

OF late years many of those most competent to give an opinion on the subject have pointed out defects of the gravest character in the system of public education prevalent in this country, not only in elementary and grammar schools, but in higher schools and colleges also. The complaint generally made is that of trying to teach too much, engaging the attention of the pupil, even of the tenderest years, on too many subjects at the same time; while the chief aim of rudimentary education should be, not to impart knowledge on all sorts of subjects, but to train the youthful mind to the habit of acquiring knowledge—to teach the art of learning, so that pupils can afterwards make the best possible use of the books they may read and the experience they may have on their way through the world.

But there is another defect in our school system that is not so often noticed or commented on. Our method of early training sins almost as much by omission as by commission. While excessive attention is devoted to some subjects, too little or none at all is given to others. Take, for instance, our system of government. How many of those leaving our grammar-schools, or even high-schools, know anything about it that is worth knowing? In some States it is not a part of the school-training at all, while in those on whose programmes it finds a place it is taught only in the most careless and superficial manner. And worse still, there is no thoroughly good text-book on the subject, the principal one that we have seen being not only superficial in its treatment, but containing several grave inaccuracies.

And on such a book as this Catholics have to depend for their knowledge, acquired during school-years, of a framework of government that should command their highest respect and admiration; for there is no other in the world that in its constitution and character so closely resembles that of the Catholic Church as does the United States Government; there is no country in which the Church enjoys more freedom than she does in ours, and there is none in which she is more prosperous. Nor has the United States any class of citizens that are more loyal to her institutions than are the Catholics.

Yet this loyalty would be more intense and widespread were a proper knowledge of the Constitution imparted to our children during the years they spend at school. They should then be made to understand the Catholic principles on which our organic law is based, and to hold it in reverence on account of these principles; to which end they need a text-book imbued with the Catholic spirit.

It is with the view to supplying such a need that the present work has been compiled; and if it aids those who read it to a clear understanding and just appreciation of its subject, the editor's wish in regard to it will be fully gratified.

CATECHISM OF THE CONSTITUTION.

CHAPTER I.

ON GOVERNMENT IN GENERAL AND ITS VARIOUS FORMS.

What is Government?

It is the ruling power in a political society.

What conception of society does this use of the word imply?

Society as moulded by the will of a sovereign or dominant body.

What is a sovereign body?

A person, or a determinate number of persons acting together, to whom the bulk of the community is habitually obedient.

How is this obedience secured?

By the enactment and enforcement of laws.

What is a Law?

A Law is a command issued by a superior to a subject, and enforced by a sanction or penalty.

Is government the same under all circumstances?

In its purpose it may be so considered; but in the manner of carrying out that purpose, no.

How do we designate the varieties of political society that have thus come into existence?

As forms of government.

Into how many classes do most writers divide these forms?

Three; namely, Monarchy, Oligarchy (or Aristocracy), and Democracy.

What is it that determines this classification?

The numerical relation between the constituent members of the government and the population of the state.

What is a Monarchy?

A state or government in which the supreme power is vested in a single person, being either limited or absolute.

When is a monarchy said to be limited?

When it is held in restraint by some other power in the state constituted for that purpose, generally called a legislature or parliament.

Of limited monarchies, which is the most conspicuous example?

That of England.

What is an absolute monarchy?

One in which no such restraint is placed upon the sovereign or sole ruler.

Does any instance of this kind of government remain in Europe?

Yes, that of Russia, and that of Turkey also.

With what form of monarchy does the earliest recorded history make us acquainted?

The patriarchal, or family government extended to whole tribes.

Where is this record to be found?

In the Pentateuch, or first five books of the Old Testament.

Who are distinctively known as the patriarchs?

Abraham, Isaac, Jacob, and the twelve sons of the last named.

How do we designate abuse of power by a monarch?

As tyranny.

Who, then, is a tyrant?

A ruler who abuses his authority by acts of oppression and cruelty.

What other power may be wielded by a monarch?
Despotism.

Who is a despot?
A ruler to whom absolute power is assigned according to the constitution of the government.

What, then, is the peculiar characteristic of a despotism?
That it exists with the consent of the governed.

What is an Aristocracy?
Government by a number of men small in proportion to the whole number of men in the state.

Is such a government known by any other name?
Yes, by that of Oligarchy, meaning "government by a few."

What meaning is commonly attributed to this word?
That of a depraved form of Aristocracy.

Where do we find examples of this form of government?
In some of the petty states of ancient Greece, and of the Italian commonwealths of the Middle Ages.

What danger most threatens an Oligarchy?
That of the political power falling into the hands of a small number of very rich and influential men, who may reduce the sphere of law to a minimum.

What is a Democracy?
It is a government controlled by a number of men large in proportion to the whole number of men in the state; so large, indeed, that the people are said to rule.

What is the best type of Democracy?
A community mainly agricultural, whose citizens, therefore, have not leisure for political affairs, and allow the law to rule.

Wherein consists the greatest danger to a democratic form of government?

In the existence of a large citizen class who have leisure for politics and are tempted to turn it to profitable account for themselves.

Which is the best government?

That in which as much as possible is left to the law, and as little as possible to the will of the governor.

By what name do we designate the absence of all government?

Anarchy.

What, then, is Anarchy?

It is a state of lawless confusion in a country.

Is there any phase of government that has not yet been mentioned?

Yes, Theocracy.

What is a Theocracy?

Government of a state by the immediate direction of God.

Where do we find an example of this form?

In the ancient Jewish state.

Have there been any imitations of it in modern times?

Yes, in the pretensions of the Puritan commonwealths of New England and the Mormon organization of Utah Territory.

What is implied by the term " Commonwealth"?

In its widest sense it means the whole body of people in a country, but in its stricter meaning it denotes a country in which a free and popular government exists.

Was it ever employed in a more limited sense?

Yes; in English history it indicates the particular government established under a Council of State after the fall of King Charles I., including also the Protectorate under Oliver Cromwell.

How is free and popular government best secured ?

By the English parliamentary, or representative, system as modified and applied in the United States.

What is there peculiar about the English system ?

Its being a combination of the three standard forms of monarchy, aristocracy, and democracy.

Has it always had the democratic element in the true sense ?

No; it has been only by slow gradations that the House of Commons has come to represent more than a fraction or a section of the people.

How and when did it become truly representative of the democracy, or the whole people?

By the Reform Act of 1885.

When did this broad and liberal system come into operation in the United States ?

With the beginning of our Government.

What body of men is it in our system that corresponds with the English House of Commons ?

The House of Representatives, or lower branch of the Congress of the United States.

Do we find in our system parallels with the other branches of the English Government ?

Yes, but in a greatly modified form.

Wherein has the greatest change been made ?

In the elimination of the hereditary principle, which in England fixes the succession to the monarchy and generally to a seat in the House of Lords.

Does the modification go any further than this ?

Yes; for a life-tenure of office we have substituted a comparatively brief term; and for hereditary succession, election by the people or by their elected representatives.

Is our system, then, a limited monarchy, like that of England?

No; it is a federal republic.

What is a Republic?

A state or country in which the supreme power is vested in rulers elected periodically by the people.

Name the oldest of existing Republics.

San Marino in Italy, Andorra in the Pyrenees, and the Swiss Cantons, all dating from the Catholic Middle Ages.

And what is a Federal Republic?

One that exists by reason of a compact or agreement between the several sovereign and co-ordinate states that compose it.

Is ours the only Federal Republic in the world?

No; Switzerland is another example.

Are there any other federal governments?

Yes; the Dominion of Canada, for instance, and the Empires of Germany and Austria also.

CHAPTER II.

THE ARTICLES OF CONFEDERATION OF THE UNITED STATES.

Which is the most illustrious example of federal government?

The United States of America.

Whence did it take its origin?

Out of the expediency, or even necessity, of a permanent and indissoluble union between the States that had thrown off the domination of England.

Why was this federation necessary instead of a complete unification?

Because of the unwillingness of the several States to abandon their individual identity and local privileges.

Was the first attempt at federation by the new States a success?

No.

And why not?

Because it was little more than an alliance offensive and defensive between States having conflicting interests, but at war with a common enemy.

How is this shown?

By the fact that no sooner was the war with England ended than disputes arose between the States that almost led to civil war.

What was the cause of this failure?

The absence of a central administrative authority to give sanction to the enactments of Congress.

By what name was the instrument of alliance known?

By that of the Articles of Confederation.

How did these Articles come into use?

By enactment of the Continental Congress, and by ratification on the part of the States.

When did Congress adopt the Articles of Confederation?

On July 9, 1778, in the beginning of "the third year of the Independence of America."

And when were they ratified by all the States?

On March 1, 1781, when Maryland gave approval.

How long did they remain in force?

Until the adoption of the present Constitution.

And why was recourse had to this instrument?

"To form a more perfect union," etc., as set forth in its preamble.

What are the essential differences between the two instruments?

They are threefold—first, as to the central authority; second, as to the constitution of the Congress; and third, as to the powers reserved to the separate States.

What of the central authority ?

Properly speaking there was none, no central administration as at present; for Congress could only recommend, and not compel, the States to carry out its enactments.

Was there not a President?

There was, but he was not vested with the authority he now has.

What was his title ?

" President of the United States in Congress assembled."

How was he chosen, and for what purpose ?

By the Congress, and to preside over its deliberations.

Was the Congress constituted in a manner similar to that by which we are now governed ?

No.

How did it differ from the present one ?

By having only one house or chamber, and by the method of regulating representation of the States.

How was State representation provided for ?

No State, no matter how small, could be represented in Congress by less than two; nor, no matter how large, by more than seven members.

Was each representative entitled to a vote ?

No; " in determining questions in the United States in Congress assembled," each State had but one vote.

Were questions decided in Congress by a mere majority ?

No; the support of nine States was required to make a measure binding on all of the thirteen.

For how long and in what manner were the delegates chosen ?

For one year only, and in such manner as the legislature of each State directed; the State even having power to recall one or all of its delegates and send others in their stead for the remainder of the year.

What restrictions were placed on persons serving as delegates in Congress ?

No person could be a delegate for more than three out of every six years; nor could he while a delegate hold any remunerative office or trust under the United States.

Whence did he derive his salary as representative ?

From the State sending him to the Congress.

Did Congress remain in session throughout the year ?

No.

Was the United States then left for a time without a central organization ?

It was not so intended; there was the Committee of the States.

How was this Committee constituted ?

It was made up of one representative from each State, but named by the Congress.

When was the Committee in authority ?

Between the adjournment of one Congress and the meeting of the next.

Did it faithfully perform the trust reposed in it ?

No; it spent most of the time in wrangling about local issues; and even on one occasion adjourned and left the country without even the semblance of a central government.

What of the authority reserved to the States ?

It was very much less limited than it has been under the Constitution.

In what respects were limitations provided for ?

In the waging of war, the maintaining of a military

force, the entering into negotiations with foreign countries, and the levying of taxes.

*Were the regulations in these regards as stringent as
at present ?*

No; they were but moderate restrictions.

*And were these restrictions complied with by the States
under all circumstances ?*

No; they were often disregarded, and this disregard
of the law increased as time went on.

Why was this ?

Because, though it was declared that "the Union
shall be perpetual," no adequate provision had been
made for punishing violations of the Articles of Confederation.

*They were not, then, "inviolably observed by every
State," as ordered by the thirteenth and last of the said
Articles ?*

On the contrary, they were so commonly disregarded
that complete nullification, nay, even war between
States, was threatened.

What evil result was actually produced ?

Business became depressed and the currency greatly
depreciated.

How was complete disruption averted ?

By a movement towards a more perfect union, which
resulted in the Constitution under which we now live.

*Was this change made in accordance with the Articles
of Confederation?*

Yes; for it was therein provided, in the thirteenth
Article, that alterations might be thereafter made in
any or all of the Articles, provided "such alteration be
agreed to in a Congress of the United States, and be
afterwards confirmed by the legislatures of every
State."

CHAPTER III.

HISTORICAL RETROSPECT.

How did the United States become an independent country ?

By joint rebellion against the tyranny of the mother country on the part of England's colonies on the Atlantic coast of North America.

When were these colonies established ?

At various times from the beginning of the seven teenth to the early part of the eighteenth century.

How many of them were there ?

Thirteen, namely: New Hampshire, Massachusetts, Rhode Island, Connecticut, New York, New Jersey, Pennsylvania, Delaware, Maryland, Virginia, North Carolina, South Carolina, and Georgia.

What was the prevailing religion in these colonies ?

Protestantism of various forms.

Were there any Catholics here ?

Yes, principally in Maryland and Pennsylvania; but scarcely any elsewhere, except a few in New Jersey and Delaware.

Were the first European settlers in America Protestants, then ?

No; Catholics had been on this continent more than a century earlier.

Who were they ?

The discoverer of the country, Columbus, and all the Spanish, Portuguese, and other explorers and colonists of his time.

Were they the first human beings to set foot on this land ?

No; they found here various peoples organized under governments more or less stable and despotic, and apparently of different races.

What do we know of these peoples?

Very little besides their condition at the time the Europeans came in contact with them. Their origin can only be surmised.

Was this native population very dense?

Only on the western part of the continent—in Mexico, Central America, and Peru (including the modern Ecuador). Towards the east it was very thin and scattered.

What would this fact seem to indicate?

That at least the greater part of the original settlers came from Asia.

Was the continent unknown to Europeans before Columbus' time?

No; it had been discovered by the Northmen at the close of the tenth or beginning of the eleventh century.

Had this discovery any lasting consequences?

No; their colonies soon became extinct, probably about the middle of the fourteenth century.

How did the continent come to be called America?

It has been generally supposed that the name was derived from *Amerigo* Vespucci, one of the explorers who followed in the wake of Columbus.

Has any other derivation been given?

Yes; recent investigations lead many to hold a different view, claiming that the word is of local origin, from *Amaraga,* a Spanish adaptation of a native name of part of the continent.

Why were the natives called Indians?

Because Columbus and others of his time thought it was a part of India they had reached.

Without Columbus, would the country have long remained unknown to Europeans?

Not likely; for, independently of him, a Portuguese

voyager, Cabral, bound for the Indies by way of the Cape of Good Hope, in the year 1500, was driven by a storm on the coast of Brazil, and for this region a claim on behalf of Portugal was set up.

What other European countries besides Spain and Portugal thus, by priority of discovery, established original claims to dominion over territory in America?

France, to the valley of the St. Lawrence, and England, to the territory of our eastern seaboard States.

When was this English claim founded?

In 1496, by Cabot, a Venetian and a Catholic, in the service of the Catholic King Henry VII.

Was this British title availed of at once?

No; not successfully for over a hundred years.

Can you account for this delay?

It was caused, probably, in the first place, by the Scotch and continental wars in which England was engaged; and, secondly, by the religious revolution begun by Henry VIII. and completed by his daughter Elizabeth.

What was the first permanent English colony here, and when was it founded?

Virginia, in the year 1607.

When were the others established?

At various intervals between this date and the year 1732.

Which of the colonies dates its beginning from this year?

Georgia, which is thus the last in point of time of the thirteen.

Did the Indians or aborigines abandon the land to the invaders?

On the contrary, they ever asserted the plenary right of dominion, which they yielded up only when they were forced to do so by the superior power of conquest, or transferred it by a voluntary cession.

What was the fundamental law of all these colonies?

The Common Law of England.

Were they all established on the same basis?

No; in this respect they were divided into three classes—namely, Provincial, Proprietary, and Charter governments.

How do you define the first-named class?

The Provincial establishments were those whose constitutions depended on the respective commissions issued by the crown to the governors, who were thus the king's deputies.

And the second?

Proprietary governments were granted out by the crown to individuals by letters-patent, these individuals thus becoming feudal lords.

And the third?

The Charter governments were in the nature of civil corporations under the immediate control of the king, who named the governor; they had the power of making by-laws for regulating their own affairs, not contrary to the laws of England.

What colonies were Provincial governments?

Virginia, New Hampshire, New York, New Jersey, the two Carolinas, and Georgia.

What Proprietary?

Maryland, Pennsylvania, and Delaware.

And which were the Charter governments?

Massachusetts (with Plymouth), Rhode Island (with Providence), and Connecticut (with New Haven).

Why is it important to keep these distinctions in mind?

Because even to the present day they affect legislation and the practice of law in the various States of our Union.

What was the religious policy of the colonies ?

It was generally that of intolerance towards all denominations but the ruling sect.

Which colony was the most prominent exception to this rule ?

Maryland, during the first or Catholic period of its existence, where there was general toleration and equality for all Christians.

What does Judge Story say of this policy of the Catholic Proprietary ?

That it was very honorable to his liberality and public spirit.

How were Catholics treated here after they became the minority ?

Those to whom they afforded protection and shelter persecuted them, their churches were closed, and they themselves were excluded from office.

In what other colonies was religious toleration practised ?

In Pennsylvania, Delaware, New Jersey, and Rhode Island.

Was it extended equally in all ?

No; Catholics were excepted both in Rhode Island and in New Jersey.

How did they fare in Pennsylvania ?

They had liberty to practise their religion as they pleased, but after 1689 were deprived of some civil rights.

What was the general attitude of the colonies towards one another before the Revolution ?

It was generally a condition of mutual rivalry and jealousy.

*How did the mother country regard this state of af-
fairs ?*

With satisfaction; and she even encouraged it·so as
to prevent a union among the colonies.

Was such a union ever attempted ?

Yes, repeatedly, and by the New England colonies
effected as early as 1643, by reason of common sym-
pathies, and to guard against danger from the sur-
rounding Indians.

How long did this confederacy last ?

Until 1686, when it was dissolved by a commission
from King James II., which also ordered the charters
of the New England colonies to be annulled.

*When was the next significant attempt at a union
made ?*

In 1722, when a congress of governors and commissioners from other colonies as well as those of New
England was held at Albany.

*Can you mention a still more interesting gathering
held in the middle of the eighteenth century?*

Yes, one that was held in the year 1754 to consider
the best means of defending America in case of the
impending war with France.

What States sent commissioners to this congress?

New Hampshire, Massachusetts, Rhode Island,
Connecticut, New York, Pennsylvania, and Maryland.

In what respect was it peculiarly remarkable ?

In the fact that the commissioners, among whom
were some of the most distinguished names in our
colonial history, asserted and promulgated truths that
prepared the way for their future independence and
our present greatness.

How is this shown ?

By the resolution which the convention unanimously adopted, that a union of all the colonies, from New Hampshire to Georgia, was absolutely necessary for their preservation.

Did the desired result follow ?

No; the people of the various colonies were too exasperated against one another about boundaries and charter claims.

Was there then any prospect of a union ?

On the contrary, it was so improbable that Dr. Franklin remarked in 1760 that a union of the colonies against the mother country was absolutely impossible unless it were forced by the most grievous tyranny and oppression.

Had the congress of 1754, then, no beneficial result?

Yes, it impressed the great value of a federated union of the Colonies on men's minds.

How soon was another congress held ?

In 1765, when, upon the recommendation of Massachusetts, a congress of delegates from nine colonies assembled at New York.

What was the chief subject of their deliberations ?

They considered a bill of rights in which the sole power of taxation was declared to reside in their own colonial legislatures.

Did anything come of this action ?

Besides bringing about the repeal of obnoxious taxes, it prepared the way for a more extensive and general association of the colonies.

When did this take place ?

In September, 1774, at the suggestion of Massachusetts.

For what is this congress remarkable ?

It laid the foundations of our independence and permanent glory by promulgating a more ample Bill of Rights, the one known specially as such in history.

By what name is this Congress called ?
By that of the First Continental Congress.
Who composed it ?
Delegates from all of the twelve colonies that were spread over the continent between Nova Scotia and Georgia.
What was it that spurred them to such an unusual course of action ?
Aggravated exactions of taxation without representation, and other exorbitant claims on the part of the British Parliament.
Did this Congress exceed its authority ?
No; instructed and directed " to meet and consult together for the common welfare," and taking into consideration the afflicted state of the country, the delegates asserted what they deemed to be the inalienable rights of freemen.
How did they specify their complaints ?
By showing to the people the system of violence which was being prepared against these rights.
To what did they pledge their constituents ?
They bound them by the sacred ties of honor and their country to renounce commerce with Great Britain.
How were these resolutions received by the people ?
With prompt and universal obedience.
Was the union thus formed continued ?
Yes; we may truly say that the Bill of Rights was the birth of American independence, the immortal Declaration that followed being its baptism.
What else at this time roused the anger of the colonies against England ?
The Quebec Act, granting full religious and political liberty to the Catholics of Canada.

Was the Revolution, then, anti-Catholic in its beginning?
Yes; at least in New England.
Did the Catholics in the rebellious colonies resent this feeling ?
No; on the contrary, when the war came even a larger proportion of them than of other denominations joined the patriot armies.
Were there any Catholic Tories ?
Only a few. During the British occupation of Philadelphia an English Catholic named Alfred Clifton tried to organize a Catholic regiment there for the British army, but he utterly failed.
Were Catholics with the patriots from the beginning?
Yes; for the leading Catholic then in Philadelphia, and almost the only one of independent means there, George Meade, was one of the signers of the non-importation resolutions of 1765.
When was the Second Continental Congress held ?
In May of the year 1775.
How were the delegates empowered to act ?
They were clothed by their constituents with ample discretionary powers, and instructed to " concert, agree upon, direct, order, and prosecute such measures as they should deem most fit and proper to obtain redress of American grievances."
Were all the colonies represented at these two congresses ?
No; Georgia had no delegates there, but soon after the latter met she acceded to and completed the confederacy of the thirteen colonies.
When and how did these colonies completely sever their connection with England and assume a separate and equal station among the nations of the earth ?
On July 4, 1776, by the ever memorable Declaration of Independence.

Did any Catholic sign this manifesto ?

Yes; Charles Carroll of Carrollton, one of Maryland's delegates, who thereby, it is said, put more wealth at stake than all the other signers together.

What other eminent service did he render to his country ?

He went on a special mission to Canada, accompanied by his cousin, Rev. John Carroll, afterwards Bishop and Archbishop of Baltimore, to enlist that colony's aid.

CHAPTER IV.

THE CONFEDERATION AND THE CONSTITUTION.

Besides the Declaration and the waging of war against England, what other step did the delegates of 1776 take towards maintaining their new station ?

The Congress, on June 11, 1776, undertook to prepare and digest articles of confederation, so as to define with precision, and by a formal instrument, the nature of the new compact, the powers of Congress, and the residuary sovereignty of the States.

Was this end speedily reached ?

No; owing to the various difficulties of the times, the state of warfare and the remnants of sectional jealousies, it was not until November 15, 1777, that Congress could agree to the Articles of Confederation.

Were these articles at once ratified by the State legislatures ?

Far from it; the same difficulties here presented themselves. Most of the States accepted the articles out of accommodation only on account of the necessities of the times.

Which were the last States to accede to them?

Delaware, in 1779, and Maryland, not until March 1, 1781.

What then became of the Continental Congress?

It was dissolved.

What became of the powers it had assumed of sovereignty necessary to maintain independence during the Revolution?

They were transmitted to the Confederation, its legally constituted successor.

Are we to think any the less of the two laggard States on account of their reluctance to enter the Confederation?

Not reasonably; for their citizens shed their blood as freely for American independence as did those of any other State.

Did the result justify the suspicions of those reluctant to give assent?

Fully; no sooner was the war ended than the defects of the compact were made obvious in several respects, especially in the impossibility of giving sanction and effect to financial and military legislation, and even to the other laws.

What followed?

A state of national degradation was threatened.

And how was this danger averted from the infant Republic?

By the calling of a Constitutional Convention to remedy the defective code.

By what State was the initiative taken?

By Virginia, whose legislature made a proposition in January, 1786, for a convention of delegates from the several States to regulate our commerce with foreign nations.

How was this proposition received?

Very favorably by several of the other States, so that five of them sent delegates to a convention which met at Annapolis in September of the same year.

What important action did they take?

They made a strong appeal to Congress for a general convention that would devise such provisions as should be proper to render the Federal Government not the mere phantom that it was, but a real government adequate to the exigencies of the Union.

Did Congress act on this suggestion?

Yes, promptly; seeing its wisdom and feeling its patriotism.

What action was taken?

Congress recommended a convention of delegates from the several States, to revise, amend, and alter the Articles of Confederation.

How many of the States accepted the proposal?

All except Rhode Island, and they appointed delegates to meet in convention.

Where and when was this convention held?

In Philadelphia, from May until September, 1787.

By what name is it known in history?

It is known as the Constitutional Convention of the United States.

What was the character of the men composing it?

In them were combined the very best talents, experience, information, patriotism, probity, and character which the country afforded.

What was the advantage of this?

In the difficult circumstances of the time it was necessary that they should command universal public confidence; and they did so.

Did they accomplish the work assigned to them ?

Yes, most effectually.

What was the character of their deliberations ?

They were marked with unprecedented unanimity.

In what did their labors result ?

In the plan of government which now forms the Constitution of the United States.

When did the Constitutional Convention complete its work ?

On September 17, 1787.

How was it to become the law of the land ?

By being submitted in each separate State to a convention of delegates chosen by the people, for assent and ratification.

In what did the chief merit of this plan consist ?

In that it was laying the foundations of our national polity where alone they ought to be laid, on the broad consent of the people.

Is there any reason why Catholics should take a special interest in this Constitution ?

Yes, for in its form it approaches nearer to the Canon Law than any other such secular instrument.

How have Catholics ever accepted it ?

With the fullest gratitude towards the fathers of the country who framed it.

Were there any Catholics among these wise men ?

Yes, two of the most prudent, conservative. and patriotic of them all.

Who were they ?

Thomas FitzSimons of Pennsylvania, Philadelphia's leading merchant in his day, and Daniel Carroll of Maryland, a cousin both of Archbishop Carroll and of Charles Carroll of Carrollton, who had signed the Declaration of Independence.

On what special occasion have the Catholics of the country shown their gratitude for the Constitution ?

On that of the celebration of the centenary of its adoption, held in Philadelphia in September, 1887, in which they took a prominent part, Cardinal Gibbons pronouncing the closing prayer.

When was the new Constitution to go into effect ?

As soon as it was ratified by nine States.

When did this take place ?

Not until September, 1788, nearly a year after its adoption by the Convention.

Was this delay a disadvantage ?

No; for thus the instrument had time to undergo the severe scrutiny of full discussion, both in private circles and in public print, as well as by the illustrious statesmen who composed the local conventions.

Which was the ninth State to ratify it ?

New Hampshire, to which thus belongs the honor of first giving it effect.

Did it then become binding on all the States ?

No; only on those so ratifying it.

When was the Government organized under the new order ?

On March 4, 1789.

Had any other States but the nine already referred to ratified the Constitution by this time ?

Yes, two more; namely, Virginia and New York, which had given their assent a few days only after New Hampshire.

What two had yet withheld their assent ?

North Carolina and Rhode Island.

When was the union of the original thirteen colonies completed ?

Not until more than a year later, namely, in June, 1790, by the acquiescence of Rhode Island.

Has the fundamental law thus framed been a success?

Yes, so much so that in a hundred years it has needed very little change.

Have not many amendments to it been made?

Yes, fifteen; but they are for the most part merely explanations and additions.

CHAPTER V.

PREAMBLE AND PLAN OF THE CONSTITUTION.

What are the component parts of the Constitution as originally adopted?

An introductory paragraph, or the Preamble, and seven Articles.

What is the purpose of the Preamble?

Merely to state the reasons for adopting the Constitution.

What were these reasons or objects?

They were, in the very words of the paragraph, 1st, to form a more perfect union; 2d, to establish justice; 3d, to insure domestic tranquillity; 4th, to provide for the common defence; 5th, to promote the general welfare; and 6th, to secure the blessings of liberty to the people and to their posterity.

Why should we dwell specially on the Preamble?

Because, in order properly to interpret the principles of the Constitution, we should bear in mind the purposes for which it was adopted.

What else does it contain?

A statement of the parties establishing the Constitution.

Who were these parties ?

The People of the United States.

How does the Constitution differ in this respect from the Articles of Confederation ?

In that the latter emanated from the States, and not directly from the people.

What else do these words of the Preamble show ?

The foundation or authority on which the Constitution is based.

Repeat the Preamble.

"We, the People of the United States, in order to form a more perfect union, establish justice, insure domestic tranquillity, provide for the common defence, promote the general welfare, and secure the blessings of liberty to ourselves and our posterity, do ordain and establish this Constitution for the United States of America."

Does this Preamble enlarge the powers of the General Government or any of its departments ?

No; it can never amount, by implication, to an enlargement of any power expressly given, nor be the legitimate source of any implied power, when otherwise withdrawn from the Constitution.

What is its true office, then ?

To expound the nature, extent, and application of the powers actually conferred by the Constitution, and not to create them.

How are these powers of government divided and classified according to our Constitution ?

Under three heads; namely, the Legislative, Executive, and Judicial powers.

What are the functions of these three powers ?

That of the Legislative is to make laws; of the Executive, to carry these laws into effect; and of the Judicial, fo interpret them when a doubt arises as to their meaning.

Should these powers be vested in the same agency or kept separate ?

The necessities of good government require their separation, for their union generally leads to. abuse of power, as has always been seen in the case of despotic or absolute governments.

How is the division or distribution of these powers provided for in our Constitution ?

They are most carefully kept separate and distinct, the details of each being treated of in a separate Article.

What are these Articles ?

Article I., which treats of the Legislative; Article II., of the Executive, and Article III., of the Judicial power.

CHAPTER VI.

THE LEGISLATIVE BRANCH OF GOVERNMENT.

How is the first Article subdivided ?

Into ten sections.

What is the purport of the first section ?

The granting and vesting of legislative powers.

Why ought the line of separation between this power and the other branches of the Government be marked with most careful and distinct precision ?

Because it is the supreme power in the state, and the department in which it resides naturally has a preponderance in the political system.

In what body in our system are legislative powers vested ?

In a Congress of the United States.

Of what does this Congress consist ?

Of a Senate and House of Representatives.

Why was the legislative body thus divided into two branches ?

That one might act as a check upon the other, thus preventing hasty and partisan legislation, at least to a great extent.

When may the plan fail of its intention ?

When the same political party has a strong majority in both branches.

Has it succeeded ?

Yes, so fairly well that some States, having originally the one-branch system, have abandoned it for the other.

Can you mention any of these States ?

Pennsylvania, before the adoption of the Constitution of 1838, and Georgia, also, had this system.

How did it work ?

Their proceedings were so marked by instability and passion as to be made the subject of much public animadversion.

What are the words of the first section of Article I. of the United States Constitution ?

> "All legislative powers herein granted shall be vested in a Congress of the United States, which shall consist of a Senate and House of Representatives."

CHAPTER VII.

THE HOUSE OF REPRESENTATIVES.

Of what does the second section of Article I. treat?
Of the House of Representatives, or lower branch of
Congress.

Is it a simple section like the first?
No; it is subdivided into five clauses.

Of what do these treat respectively?
The first, of the membership of the House; the second, of the qualification of Representatives; the third,
of the apportionment of Representatives, and taxes
according to numbers; the fourth, of the filling of
vacancies; and the fifth, of the powers of the House.

Repeat Clause 1.
  "The House of Representatives shall be composed of members chosen every second year
  by the people of the several States; and the
  electors in each State shall have the qualifications requisite for electors of the most numerous branch of the State legislature."

What is the purport of this clause?
The composition of the House and the qualification
of those choosing its members.

*How long is the term for which members of the House
are chosen?*
Two years. The whole House is renewed every
second year.

*Why was this rule of a comparatively short term of
service adopted?*
In order that the people might have more frequent

opportunity of expressing approval or disapproval of their Representatives' conduct.

Who choose them?

The voters of the various States, by States.

Why was it necessary to say that "the electors in each State shall have the qualifications requisite for electors of the most numerous branch of the State legislature?"

Because different franchise laws prevailed in different States, and have so prevailed down to our time.

Can you mention one very peculiar instance?

That of Rhode Island, where a law requiring a property qualification for citizens of foreign birth was repealed only by the legislature of 1888, the new law taking effect only in 1889.

As a general rule who are electors?

All male native citizens of over twenty-one years, and all those of foreign birth who have been duly naturalized.

Is full naturalization required in every instance?

No; in some States the franchise is given to men who have merely declared intention to become citizens.

What qualifications must a man possess to become a member of the House?

Those set forth in Clause 2 of the second section of Article I., as follows:

"No person shall be a representative who shall not have attained to the age of twenty-five years, and been seven years a citizen of the United States, and shall not, when elected, be an inhabitant of that State in which he shall be chosen."

How old must a man be to become a Representative in Congress?
At least twenty-five years.
How long a citizen of the United States?
At least seven years.
And what is the third qualification he must possess?
He must, when elected, be an inhabitant of the State sending him to Congress.
Must he reside in the district he wishes to represent?
No; congressional districts are only of comparatively recent institution.

CHAPTER VIII.

APPORTIONMENT OF THE REPRESENTATIVES IN CONGRESS.

To what does Clause 3 of the same section refer?
To the apportionment of Representatives and direct taxes among the States according to their population.
Does this clause stand now as it was originally framed?
No; a portion of it has been changed by an amendment adopted soon after the close of our civil war.
What led to this change?
The abolition of slavery in all the States of the Union.
Were slaves, then, not counted in the population of the States in which they lived?
Not fully, as regarded representation of those States in Congress.
To what extent, then?
For the purpose of representation three-fifths only

of the slaves were added to the number of free persons.

Did these slaves enjoy the franchise?

No; they only entitled the States to more members of the House of Representatives than they would have had without them.

Besides the remaining two-fifths of slaves, were there any inhabitants not counted?

Yes; all Indians not taxed.

What of persons bound to service for a term of years?

They were counted among the whole number of free persons.

Who were meant by those bound to service for a number of years?

Apprentices, who were therefore included among the number of free persons.

Repeat the portion of the third clause treating of these matters.

" Representatives and direct taxes shall be apportioned among the several States which may be included within this Union according to their respective numbers, which shall be determined by adding to the whole number of free persons, including those bound to service for a term of years, and, excluding Indians not taxed, three-fifths of all other persons.

By what enactment are parts of these regulations modified?

By the Fourteenth Amendment to the Constitution.

What is the next sentence of this Clause 3?

" The actual enumeration shall be made within three years after the first meeting of Congress, and within every subsequent term of ten years, in such manner as they shall by law direct."

When was this part of our fundamental law first complied with ?

In the year 1790.

Has it been fully carried out since ?

Yes; regularly once every ten years.

Did the Constitution limit the number of representatives ?

It did.

How were they limited ?

They were not to exceed one for every thirty thousand inhabitants.

What of a State whose population was less than thirty thousand ?

It was to have one representative in Congress.

What are the words of the Constitution making this regulation ?

"The number of Representatives shall not exceed one for every thirty thousand, but each State shall have at least one Representative."

Before the first enumeration or census was made, how many Representatives did all the States have in Congress ?

A total number of sixty-five members.

How were these members apportioned among the States?

New Hampshire had three; Massachusetts, eight; Rhode Island, one; Connecticut, five; New York, six; New Jersey, four; Pennsylvania, eight; Delaware, one; Maryland, six; Virginia, ten; North Carolina, five; South Carolina, five, and Georgia, three.

Has this proportion been changed ?

Yes, repeatedly, after each census.

Do these States still retain the same ratio of representation to one another ?

Not at all; some now have more and some less.

What States have now the same number of Representatives as they had then ?

Delaware, Maryland, and Virginia.

In what States has the number been reduced ?

In New Hampshire and Connecticut.

Where has the greatest proportion of increase taken place ?

In New York State.

How have these changes been brought about ?

By changes in the proportionate amount of population of the various States.

In what other way has the membership of the House of Representatives been changed ?

By the admission of new States into the Union.

How many of these new States have been admitted ?

Twenty-five.

May others be admitted ?

Yes; preparations are now in progress for the admission of four others, namely: North Dakota, South Dakota, Washington, and Montana.

When may they become States of the Union ?

As soon as their constitutions are approved by Congress.

Of how many States, then, is the Union now composed ?

Thirty-eight.

Under what apportionment are they now represented in Congress ?

Under that of 1882.

On what census is this apportionment based ?

On that of 1880.

Can you give the names of the thirty-eight States, and the number of members of the House of Representatives to which each is now entitled ?

Yes; they are: New York, thirty-four; Pennsylvania, twenty-eight; Ohio, twenty-one; Illinois, twenty; Missouri, fourteen; Indiana, thirteen; Massachusetts, twelve; Kentucky, Michigan, Iowa, and Texas, eleven each; Virginia, Georgia, and Tennessee, ten each; North Carolina and Wisconsin, nine each; Alabama, eight; New Jersey, South Carolina, Mississippi, and Kansas, seven each; Maryland, Louisiana, and California, six each; Arkansas and Minnesota, five each; Connecticut, Maine, and West Virginia, four each; Nebraska, three; New Hampshire, Rhode Island, Vermont, and Florida, two each; and Delaware, Oregon, Nevada, and Colorado, one each.

Of how many members, then, does the House of Representatives consist at present?

Of 325 members.

What, according to the census of 1880, is the proportion of inhabitants to each Representative?

It is 151,912.

Is this same proportion maintained in the various States?

As nearly as possible.

How do the States elect their Representatives?

By single member districts arranged according to population.

How is this done?

By act of the State Legislature.

Was this always the rule?

No; originally the voters throughout the whole State voted for as many candidates for the House of Representatives as the State was entitled to.

The division of the States into districts, each of which returns a single member, is an innovation, then?

Yes, in many States it is of comparatively recent date.

When a vacancy occurs in the representation of any State, how is it filled?

The executive authority of that State issues a writ of election to fill such vacancy.

When by apportionment of Congress an additional member is assigned to any State, and the Legislature of that State fails to make a new apportionment, how is the additional member elected?

By the voters of the whole State, or "at large," as it is called.

Repeat the clause referring to the filling of vacancies.

"When vacancies happen in the representation from any State, the executive authority thereof shall issue writs of election to fill such vacancies."

Has the House of Representatives power over its own organization?

Yes, it has power to choose the Speaker, or presiding officer, and other officers of the House.

What other power is vested in this body alone?

That of impeachment.

What does this power imply?

It implies that the Representatives have a right to bring accusation against high officials of the Government on account of improper administration of the duties of office.

Has the House the power to try impeachments also?

No; this power belongs to the Senate, as we shall see a little later on.

Repeat the clause assigning certain powers to the House.

"The House of Representatives shall choose their Speaker and other officers, and shall have the sole power of impeachment."

CHAPTER IX.

THE UNITED STATES SENATE.

What is the subject of the third section of Article I. of the Constitution?

The election, organization, and duties of the second or higher branch of the United States Congress.

By what name is this branch called?

By that of the United States Senate.

Of whom is this body composed?

Of two delegates from each State.

How are they chosen?

By the legislatures of the separate States.

For how long a term are they chosen?

For six years.

Are they all chosen for terms beginning at the same time?

No; a third of them are replaced every two years.

The organization of the Senate differs, then, from that of the House?

Yes; not only as to the number of members, but also in the mode of election and the length of the term of service.

How many members now compose the Senate?

Seventy-six.

What advantage is thought to be derived from their long term of service?

The counteracting of the influence of the fluctuations of popular opinion on the lower branch of the legislature.

What other advantage accrues ?
The smallest States have an equal voice with the largest.

How is the voting done in the Senate ?
Each Senator has one vote.

How was voting done in the Continental Congress ?
One vote was cast for each State.

Repeat the first clause of Section 3.

> "The Senate of the United States shall be composed of two Senators from each State, chosen by the Legislature thereof for six years; and each Senator shall have one vote."

How were the Senators divided originally into three sections, each third part of them going out every two years ?
By the second clause of the third section of Article I. of the Constitution it was so ordered.

What are the words ordering this division ?
They are these:

> "Immediately after they shall be assembled in consequence of the first election, they shall be divided, as equally as may be, in three classes."

What is said, then, about the vacating and filling of the seats of those of the first class ?

> "The seats of the Senators of the first class shall be vacated at the expiration of the second year."

And of those of the second class ?
> "At the expiration of the fourth year."

And of those of the third class ?
> "At the expiration of the sixth year."

How many, then, are chosen every second year ?
One-third, or as near as may be.

What is the consequence of this arrangement?
The Senate is practically made a perpetual body.
Does any advantage accrue from this?
In this way the Senate may always contain a considerable proportion of members well versed in public business.

How is a vacancy filled that happens "by resignation or otherwise during the recess of the legislature of any State"?
It is provided in the same clause that in such cases the executive of said State "may make temporary appointments until the next meeting of the legislature, which shall then fill such vacancies."

What are the qualifications requisite to become a Senator?
They are three: age, citizenship, and residence.
How old must he be?
Thirty years.
How long a citizen?
Nine years.
And what of his residence?
He must be an inhabitant of the State for which he is chosen.

Repeat the clause reciting the qualifications of Senators.
"No person shall be a Senator who shall not have attained to the age of thirty years, and been nine years a citizen of the United States, and who shall not, when elected, be an inhabitant of that State for which he shall be chosen."

How do the qualifications of a Senator differ from those of a Representative?
The latter need be only twenty-five years old and seven years a citizen.

Who ordinarily presides over the Senate?
The Vice-President of the United States.
Is he privileged to vote?
Not unless the Senate be evenly divided in voting.
Repeat the clause dealing with the Vice-President's relations to the Senate.

> "The Vice-President of the United States shall be President of the Senate, but shall have no vote, unless they be equally divided."

In case of the death or absence of the Vice-President, or when he may exercise the office of President of the United States, who presides over the Senate?
An officer specially chosen from among the Senators themselves for such an emergency, who is called the President *pro tempore* of the Senate.
How are the other officers of the Senate chosen?
By the members of that body themselves.
In what clause of Section 3 are these provisions made?
In the fifth, which reads as follows:

> "The Senate shall choose other officers, and also a President *pro tempore*, in the absence of the Vice-President, or when he shall exercise the office of President of the United States."

CHAPTER X.

IMPEACHMENT TRIALS.

What power is it that is vested in the Senate only?
The power to try all impeachments.

Wherein is the power to order an impeachment trial vested?
In the House of Representatives, as we have already seen.

How does the Senate conduct an impeachment trial?
All the Senators take part, forming a jury, and are put on oath or affirmation.

Why is this done?
Because they are then equivalent to a jury.

Who presides in ordinary cases of impeachment?
The actual President of the Senate.

Are there any exceptional cases?
Yes, one.

What is it?
When the person impeached is the President of the United States.

Who presides in this instance?
The Chief-Justice of the Supreme Court of the United States.

What is requisite for conviction in an impeachment trial?
The concurrence of two-thirds of the Senators present.

Why was this number chosen instead of a majority or a unanimous vote?
Because of the prevalence of political feeling; in the former case few would escape, and in the latter few could be convicted.

Repeat the clause relating to impeachments.
"The Senate shall have the sole power to try
all impeachments. When sitting for that
purpose they shall be on oath or affirmation.
When the President of the United States is
tried, the Chief-Justice shall preside; and no
person shall be convicted without the concurrence of two-thirds of the members present."

*To what does the seventh and last clause of this sec-
tion refer ?*
To the extent of judgment in cases of impeachment.
How far does such judgment extend ?
No "further than to removal from office, and disqualification to hold and enjoy any office of honor,
trust, or profit under the United States."
*Is the party convicted liable to trial in any other
court ?*
Yes; he may afterwards "be liable and subject to
indictment, trial, judgment, and punishment, according to law."

CHAPTER XI.

ELECTION TO AND MEETING OF CONGRESS.

What is the subject of the fourth section of Article I. ?
The manner of electing members and of the meeting
of both branches of Congress.
*In whom does the Constitution vest the power of regu-
lating these elections ?*
In the legislature of each State.

Does Congress in this regard reserve any power to itself?

Yes; that of making or altering such regulations, except as to the places for choosing Senators.

Why does it reserve this power?

Because the State legislature may neglect to make such provision, and thus embarrass or impede the progress of public business.

Why does Congress not interfere as to the place of choosing Senators?

Because it is the exclusive province of the State legislature, which chooses them, to decide where it shall meet and transact the business of the State.

What may the State legislature do in regard to the election of members of Congress?

It may choose the times, places, and manner of holding elections, except when Congress may interfere as already explained.

What are the words of the clause laying down these regulations?

"The times, places, and manner of holding elections for Senators and Representatives shall be prescribed in each State by the legislature thereof; but the Congress may at any time, by law, make or alter such regulations, except as to the places of choosing Senators."

What provision is made as to the meeting of Congress?

That it shall assemble at least once a year.

Is the time of such meeting specified?

Yes; the first Monday of December is the day named.

Is power given to change this date?

Yes; but it has never been exercised.

Repeat Clause 2 of the fourth section—that which regulates the meeting of Congress.

"The Congress shall assemble at least once in every year, and such meeting shall be on the first Monday in December, unless they shall by law appoint a different day."

When are members of the House of Representatives now generally elected?

On the Tuesday next following the first Monday of November of each even year.

Why do you say generally?

Because they are chosen at a different time in some States, namely, at the time of the State election.

Were the majority always chosen in November?

No; the rule of uniformity in this regard has been but very slowly and gradually adopted by the States.

Does the Congress meet on the first Monday of December next following the November election at which they are chosen?

No; not for a year later.

When does the term of each Congress end?

At noon on the fourth day of March of each odd year.

How many regular sessions may each Congress hold?

Two.

How are they popularly distinguished?

As the long session and the short session.

How does the latter get its name?

Because it must end on the fourth day of March, while the former may be continued until the opening of the latter.

How is any one's right to a seat in Congress ascertained?

Each House examines and passes upon the claims of those applying for membership in it.

How many members are necessary to the transaction of business?

A majority of the whole number entitled to seats in each House.

By what name is such a majority known?

It is designated a quorum.

If a smaller number meet, what may they do?

They may adjourn from day to day.

Can they compel absent members to attend?

Yes; in such manner and under such penalties as each House may provide.

Why is this power given to a minority of a legislative body?

Because if such authority were not given, a portion of the members could suspend legislation by purposely absenting themselves.

Repeat the first clause of Section 5.

"Each House shall be the judge of the elections, returns, and qualifications of its own members; and a majority of each shall constitute a quorum to do business; but a smaller number may adjourn from day to day, and may be authorized to compel the attendance of absent members, in such manner and under such penalties as each house may provide."

What provision is made for the maintenance of order in Congress?

Each House may determine its own rules.

What may be done with a member guilty of disorderly conduct?

He may receive such punishment as his fellow-members see fit to inflict, or be expelled from the House if two-thirds of them so decide.

Why was this power given?

To preserve decorum among so important a body of men.

What are the words of the clause relating to these rules of order?

> " Each House may determine the rules of its proceedings, punish its members for disorderly behavior, and with the concurrence of two-thirds expel a member."

How is a record of the proceedings to be kept?

Each House is ordered by the third clause of Section 5 to keep a journal thereof.

Is this to be published?

Yes, excepting such parts as may in the judgment of the members require secrecy.

Is the record of votes and divisions to be kept on the journal?

Yes, if one-fifth of those present demand that the yeas and nays be recorded.

What is meant by taking the yeas and nays?

Recording the names of those voting and the side on which they vote.

Have both Houses of Congress always held open sessions?

No; in the first few years of its history all the sessions of the Senate were held in secret.

Has the practice been entirely abandoned?

No; occasionally the Senate still holds secret sessions.

When may Congress adjourn?

Only when both Houses have agreed to do so can they terminate a session.

Can either House adjourn temporarily?

Yes, but for no longer than three days without the consent of the other.

Is there a limit as to the place of adjournment?

They cannot adjourn to any other place than that in which the two Houses shall be sitting.

What is the clause regarding adjournment?

It is the fourth and last of Section 5 of Article I.

How does it run?

"Neither House, during the session of Congress, shall, without the consent of the other, adjourn for more than three days, nor to any other place than that in which the two Houses shall be sitting."

CHAPTER XII.

SALARIES, PRIVILEGES, AND DISABILITIES OF MEMBERS OF CONGRESS.

What is the subject of the next section?

The salaries, privileges, and disabilities of Members of Congress.

What is provided as to salaries?

That "the Senators and Representatives shall receive a compensation for their services."

How is this compensation to be determined?

It is "to be ascertained by law."

How much compensation do Senators receive?

Five thousand dollars a year.

How much does the President of the Senate, or Vice-President of the United States, get?

Eight thousand dollars a year.

What is the salary of members of the House of Representatives?

Five thousand dollars a year.

And that of the Speaker of the House?

Eight thousand dollars a year.

Whence is this money to be drawn?

Out of the Treasury of the United States.

What are the special privileges of members of both Houses?

Exemption from arrest and from responsibility for speeches made in either House outside of the place in which they have been delivered.

How far does the exemption from arrest extend?

To the time while they are attending at the session of their respective Houses, or while they are going to or returning from the same.

Is there any exception to this rule?

Yes; even during this privileged time they may be arrested for treason, felony, and breach of the peace.

What do you think of the three principal rulings of this clause?

They are all based on wisdom.

Is it well to pay members a competent salary?

Yes; for while it may in some cases tempt unworthy persons to seek the office, yet it opens the way for others than the wealthy, and thus does away with limiting law-making to a privileged class, as has always been the case in England.

Why should members be exempted from arrest?

Because otherwise constituencies might be left unrepresented in Congress, and public business might suffer detriment.

Are the exceptions to this exemption based on sound judgment?

Yes; for thus a safeguard is placed over the conduct of the members.

And what is the advantage of holding them responsible for their speeches only in the respective Houses in which these speeches may be delivered ?

That entire freedom of debate, combined with decorum of language, may be preserved.

Repeat, then, the first clause of Section 6.

"The Senators and Representatives shall receive a compensation for their services, to be ascertained by law, and paid out of the Treasury of the United States. They shall in all cases, except treason, felony, and breach of the peace, be privileged from arrest during their attendance at the session of their respective Houses, and in going to and returning from the same; and for any speech or debate in either House they shall not be questioned in any other place."

What is the subject of the other clause of this section ?

The disability to hold offices.

From what offices are Senators and Representatives excluded during their term of service in either House ?

From such civil offices under the authority of the United States as may be created or whose emoluments may be increased during such time.

Can persons holding office under the United States become Members of Congress ?

Not unless they resign from such offices.

Can Members of Congress be appointed to offices under the United States Government already existing ?

They can, provided the emoluments of these offices have not been increased during their term in Congress.

Why are Members of Congress excluded from such offices ?

Because otherwise, in the hope of pecuniary gain,

they might, without any other reason, be induced to vote for the creation of such offices.

What must a Member of Congress do before accepting an office under the United States?

He must first resign his seat in Congress.

And what if an office-holder wants to become a Member of Congress?

He must resign his office.

Repeat Clause 2 of the sixth section.

"No Senator or Representative shall, during the time for which he was elected, be appointed to any civil office under the authority of the United States which shall have been created, or the emoluments whereof shall have been increased, during such time; and no person holding any office under the United States shall be a member of either House during his continuance in office."

What power is vested in the House which the Senate does not possess?

That of originating bills for the raising of revenue.

Has the Senate, then, nothing to do with such bills?

Yes; it may pass upon them as upon other bills, and propose amendments to them.

Where is this provision made?

It is found in the first clause of the seventh section of Article I.

How does this clause read?

As follows:

"All bills for raising revenue shall originate in the House of Representatives; but the Senate may propose or concur with amendments as on other bills."

CHAPTER XIII.

THE ENACTMENT OF LAWS.

How does a bill become a law ?

It must first be adopted in exactly the same words by both Houses, and then be approved by the President of the United States.

How does he give a bill the force of law ?

Either by signing it with his name as President, or allowing a certain period to elapse without acting upon it at all.

How may he prevent a bill from becoming a law ?

By "vetoing" it.

What is meant by vetoing ?

His returning it without his signature, and with a statement of his objections to it, to the House in which it originated.

What does this House then do with it ?

It orders the objections to be entered at large upon the journal of the House, and proceeds to reconsider it.

After this, may the bill yet become a law ?

Yes, if, upon such reconsideration, two-thirds of the votes of both Houses are recorded in favor of it.

Is it then sent again to the President for his signature ?

No; it now becomes a law without his signing it.

What is this process called ?

It is known as passing a bill over the President's veto.

In case it fails to receive a two-thirds vote in either House after being sent back vetoed, what becomes of it ?

It is at once dropped from further consideration.

What are the words of the Constitution relating to the signing and vetoing of bills by the President?

" Every bill which shall have passed the House of Representatives and the Senate shall, before it become a law, be presented to the President of the United States; if he approve, he shall sign it; but if not, he shall return it, with his objections, to that House in which it shall have originated, who shall enter the objections at large on their journal, and proceed to reconsider it. If, after such reconsideration, two-thirds of that House shall agree to pass the bill, it shall be sent, together with the objections, to the other House, by which it shall likewise be reconsidered, and if approved by two-thirds of that House, it shall become a law."

How are the votes determined in such cases ?

By recording the yeas and nays; that is, taking down the names of those voting for and against.

Are these names thus taken down entered on the journals ?

Yes, on that of each House respectively.

How is this provision stated in the fundamental law ?

" In all cases the votes of both Houses shall be determined by yeas and nays, and the names of the persons voting for and against the bill shall be entered on the journal of each House respectively."

In what other way than by passing over the President's veto can a bill become a law without his signature?

By remaining in his hands ten days (not counting Sundays), while Congress is in session, without his taking any action upon it.

Why do we say "while Congress is in session"?

Because, should Congress adjourn before the expiration of the ten days, then it does not become a law.

What is the language of the Constitution in reference to this wise ruling?

"If any bill shall not be returned by the President within ten days (Sundays excepted) after it shall have been presented to him, the same shall be a law in like manner as if he had signed it, unless the Congress by their adjournment prevented its return, in which case it shall not be a law."

To what is the last clause of the seventh section devoted?

To the forms of procedure on joint resolutions.

What is their general character?

These forms are in general the same as those laid down for the enacting of laws.

Are they not the same in all cases?

No; there is one exception.

What is this exception?

The motion or joint resolution of both Houses to adjourn.

Has the President the veto power over all other resolutions?

Yes, just the same as in the case of ordinary bills.

Why was this power given to him?

In order to prevent laws from being enacted in the form of joint resolutions.

Repeat the clause regarding these resolutions.
   " Every order, resolution, or vote to which the
      concurrence of the Senate and House of
      Representatives may be necessary (except on
      a question of adjournment) shall be presented
      to the President of the United States, and
      before the same shall take effect shall be ap-
      proved by him, or, being disapproved by him,
      shall be repassed by two-thirds of the Senate
      and House of Representatives, according to
      the rules and limitations prescribed in the
      case of a bill."

CHAPTER XIV.

TAXATION.

Of what does the eighth section of Article I. treat ?
Of the powers granted to Congress.
How are these powers enumerated ?
They are set forth in seventeen different clauses.
Which of these powers is mentioned first ?
That of taxation.
What is a tax ?
Money which the law requires individual citizens to
pay towards the meeting of public expenses.
How many kinds of taxes are there ?
Two; direct and indirect taxes.
What is a direct tax ?
Such as is levied upon and collected from the citi-
zen either on account of his person or his property.
How many kinds of direct taxes are there, then ?
Two also, as we see from the preceding answer:
those upon persons and those upon property.

Is the power of levying these taxes confined to the Federal Government?

No; they may be levied also by the State governments.

By what other names is the personal tax known?

It is sometimes called poll tax and sometimes capitation tax.

What are indirect taxes?

Those levied and depending on the consumption of certain articles of commerce.

How many kinds of indirect taxes are there?

Three; namely, those on imports, exports, and manufactures.

What are imports?

Goods brought into the country from abroad.

What are exports?

Goods sent out of the country to other countries.

And what is meant here by manufactures?

Goods produced in the country.

What name is given to taxes on imported goods?

Imposts.

And what names apply to taxes on both imported and exported goods?

Customs and duties.

What is the place called where these taxes are levied?

The Custom-house.

What is the common name given to taxes on manufactures?

The excise.

How are direct taxes apportioned among the States?

In the same manner as are Representatives in Congress; namely, according to the relative population of the States.

What power is vested in Congress in regard to taxation ?

The power "to lay and collect taxes, duties, imposts, and excises."

What else is laid down in the Constitution regarding these taxes ?

That "all duties, imposts, and excises shall be uniform throughout the United States."

Where are these regulations set forth ?

In the first clause of the eighth section of Article I.

What other direction is given in this same clause ?

That Congress shall "pay the debts and provide for the common defence and general welfare of the United States."·

What would seem to have been the intention of the framers of the Constitution in combining these two statements together ?

That only so much taxes should be levied as are necessary to meet the expenses of government.

Repeat the whole clause.

"The Congress shall have power to lay and collect taxes, imposts, and excises; to pay the debts and provide for the common defence and general welfare of the United States; but all duties, imposts, and excises shall be uniform throughout the United States."

What is the next power expressly given to Congress ?

"To borrow money on the credit of the United States."

Why is it necessary for Congress to have this power ?

Because on it depends not only the credit, but the existence of the Federal Government, in a time of great exigency, when taxes could not be levied soon enough or plentifully enough.

CHAPTER XV.

COMMERCE.

What is the subject of the third clause ?

The regulating of commerce with foreign nations, between the States of the Union, and with the Indian tribes.

What is meant by these words ?

The laying down of rules by which the carrying on of commerce is to be governed.

What two ideas are combined in the name of commerce ?

Those of navigation and of traffic, or interchange of commodities.

Does this clause give Congress any special privileges within the individual States ?

Yes; it gives Congress absolute control over all navigable waters, not only along the coast and between separate States, but even within the limits of any State.

What duties follow this right ?

The surveying of coasts and harbors, the clearing of channels, the building and maintenance of light-houses and quarantine stations, etc.

Has Congress any other duties to perform in regard to the shipping trade ?

It enacts laws regarding seamen on American vessels, concerning fisheries and the coasting trade, pilotage laws, etc.

How does government under the Constitution differ in respect to commerce laws from the old Confederacy ?

Not only the Confederation, but the Continental

Congress preceding it, had no power over commerce, the regulation and management of which was left to each particular State.

What came of this state of affairs ?

The almost total decay and destruction of the shipping trade of the States, and the springing up of rivalries and jealousies between them that brought them almost to civil war.

With whom now do the Indian tribes deal and negotiate ?

With the United States Government.

With whom did they deal before the Revolution ?

With the ruling authority in the various colonies acting in the name of the King of England.

Has the Congress power to regulate commerce between the States ?

Yes; and is now exercising this power by means of the Inter-State Commerce Act.

CHAPTER XVI.

NATURALIZATION.

Of what does the fourth clause of the section under consideration treat ?

Of the two subjects of naturalization and bankruptcy.

Has Congress always exercised its privilege in regard to these matters ?

Only in the most general way; the various States have been allowed to make laws regulating the details of both.

What does naturalization mean?

Giving the rights of citizenship to foreigners taking up a permanent residence in this country.

Is it important that the conditions of citizenship should be the same for all the States?

Yes; a citizen of one State is entitled by the Constitution to all the rights of citizenship in every State of the Union.

Have the States given a uniform interpretation to this right?

No; in Pennsylvania, for instance, a foreigner must have completed his naturalization before he can be permitted to practise law, while, according to a recent decision in New York, he need only declare his intention to become a citizen in order that he be admitted to the bar.

There are, then, different stages in the process of naturalization?

Yes, two; the declaration of intention to become a citizen, and the carrying into effect of this intention.

When may the declaration of intention be made?

At any time after arrival in the country.

And when may naturalization take place?

Not sooner than after five years of continuous residence here, and at least two full years after the declaration of intention has been made.

Has this always been the law under our Constitution?

No, though it was the law originally adopted.

When was the original law changed?

In 1798, during the administration of President Adams.

What was the nature of the change?

It required a term of twenty-one years' residence as a condition of citizenship for foreigners.

How long did this law remain in force ?
Nearly five years.

When was it repealed ?
In the early part of Jefferson's first administration.

Has the law been interfered with since ?
No; though there has repeatedly been agitation in favor of the longer term of probation.

Do you remember the two most noteworthy instances of this agitation ?
They were the Native-American movement of 1844 and the Know-Nothing movement of 1855.

What is the best-known outcome of citizenship ?
The electoral franchise, or privilege of voting.

Has this always been uniform in all the States ?
By no means, and complete uniformity has not yet been reached, though the tendency has ever been in this direction.

What State presents the most noteworthy exception to the rule ?
Rhode Island, where a property qualification was long required of citizens of foreign birth.

Has not this law been repealed ?
Yes, but it took effect only in 1889.

Is there any other discrepancy between the States as to voting ?
Yes, and in the direction of extreme liberality.

What is this ?
For the exercise of the electoral franchise only the declaration of intention and a short term of residence is required in as many as fifteen States.

What are these States ?
Alabama, Arkansas, Colorado, Florida, Indiana, Kansas, Louisiana, Michigan, Minnesota, Mississippi, Nebraska, Nevada, Oregon, Texas, and Wisconsin.

How do some try to reconcile this state of affairs with the provision in the United States Constitution making naturalization uniform for all the States ?

By simply declaring that the electoral franchise is a privilege separate and apart from citizenship.

What are the words of the Constitution in this regard ?

"The Congress shall have power to establish a uniform rule of naturalization."

CHAPTER XVII.

BANKRUPTCY LAWS, THE CURRENCY, COPYRIGHT, AND PATENTS.

Is a similar provision made as to bankruptcy ?

Yes; it is enacted that there may be "uniform laws on the subject of bankruptcies throughout the United States."

What provisions should be made by bankrupt and insolvent laws ?

Creditors should be secured as far as possible when their debtors become insolvent.

How far should this security extend ?

The insolvent debtor's effects should be fully surrendered and equitably distributed among the creditors.

What right should be secured to unfortunate debtors ?

Their creditors, after getting their surrender, should give them a legal discharge.

Is it wise to give creditors power to imprison well-meaning debtors or to establish a claim on their future earnings ?

No; because this course would lead the debtor to despondency or tempt him to dishonesty.

Does the obligation to pay debts cease when the debtor is discharged ?

No; if he afterwards acquires the means, he is bound in conscience to pay as much of his former obligations as he can.

Has the uniformity as to a national bankruptcy law recommended by the framers of the Constitution ever been adopted ?

Yes, but only occasionally and for brief periods.

When were these ?

From 1801 to 1803, from 1842 to 1843, and from 1866 to 1879.

In what condition, then, are the bankruptcy laws at present ?

Each State has its own bankruptcy laws.

Has Congress any other powers over the financial affairs of the country ?

Yes; it has power to coin money and to regulate its value, as well as the value of the coined money of other countries that may be brought into this country.

What is the advantage of giving this power to Congress ?

It greatly simplifies business relations between the States.

What other power vested in Congress tends in the same direction ?

The fixing of the standard of weights and measures.

Is any precaution taken against counterfeiting the current coin of the United States ?

Yes; Congress is given power to provide for the punishment of those undertaking such counterfeiting.

What is a coin ?

A piece of metal, of a determined shape, size, and weight, stamped so as to represent a certain value.

What metals are used for this purpose in the United States ?

Gold, silver, nickel, and copper.

Are all these of the standard of legal tender ?

No; only gold and silver can be tendered in payment of debt to the United States.

Are there any other devices in current use for representing values ?

Yes, bank-notes, including those issued by the United States Treasury.

Is it a crime to counterfeit or imitate these ?

Yes, just the same as the making of spurious coins.

By what common name are coins and bank-notes known ?

By that of money.

What is the name of the place where hard money is made or coined ?

The Mint.

What are the words of the Constitution regarding coinage and weights and measures ?

"The Congress shall have power to coin money, regulate the value thereof, and of foreign coin, and fix the standard of weights and measures; to provide for the punishment of counterfeiting the securities and current coin of the United States."

How is Congress enabled to facilitate communication between different parts of the country ?

By the power given to it in the Constitution to establish post-offices and post-roads.

What special advantage accrues from this regula-. tion ?

The more regular, speedy, and secure transmission of messages and of money.

Besides this general security, what special protection is afforded to certain citizens ?

To authors and inventors is secured for a certain period the profits accruing from their writings and inventions.

Why is this done ?

To promote and encourage progress in the sciences and useful arts.

What are these rights called ?

Copyright and patent-right.

How is copyright secured ?

By application to the Librarian of Congress.

How is a patent-right secured ?

By application to the Patent Office in Washington.

Who may apply for these rights ?

Either the authors and inventors, or those who may have purchased their claims.

For how long may copyright on a book be secured ?

For twenty-eight years.

May this right be renewed ?

Yes, for fourteen years longer.

How long does a patent-right run ?

For fourteen years.

May this right be renewed ?

No ; but any improvement may also be patented.

CHAPTER XVIII.

PIRACY, WARFARE, AND MILITARY REGULATIONS.

Can Congress constitute courts of justice other than those provided for in the Constitution?

Yes, it can constitute tribunals inferior to the Supreme Court, and make regulations for punishing piracies and felonies committed on the high seas, and offences against the law of nations.

What is an act of piracy?

A robbery committed on the high seas.

What is the limit or boundary of the high seas?

Low-water mark.

Why do not the States punish such crimes committed within their borders?

Because all navigable waters in the States belong to the United States.

What is the punishment for piracy or felony committed at sea?

The death penalty.

Why is punishment for offences against the law of nations assigned to the United States Government?

Because it, and not an individual State of the Union, is responsible to foreign governments.

In what branch of our Government is vested the right of declaring war?

In the legislative branch, or Congress.

How does our Government differ in this respect from most other governments?

In others, especially monarchies, such power belongs to the Executive.

Why is our system to be preferred?

Because with us it rests directly with the people to say whether they shall go to war or not.

Is not this the case with monarchies?

No; the people living under monarchies are expected to do what their rulers command.

Why should the people have the chief voice in such a serious matter?

Because they have to bear the expenses.

What right may be delegated to private citizens in time of war?

The right to capture the property of citizens of a hostile nation.

What process is required in conferring this right?

The issuing of "letters of marque and reprisal" to such citizens.

By what name are persons receiving such commissions known?

By that of privateers.

Are "letters of marque and reprisal" issued at other times than when this country may be engaged in war?

Occasionally, if it should happen that a citizen is injured by another country and has no other means of redress.

To what extent can reprisal in such a case be made?

Only to the extent of the injury done.

What other regulations may Congress make for times of war?

Rules concerning captures on land and water.

Has Congress no other powers in military matters on such occasions?

Yes, it can raise armies and provide for their support.

For an indefinite period?

No, only for a period of two years or less.

Why is this restriction placed on Congress ?

So that no standing army may be maintained in time of peace unless the people give their assent thereto.

Is there a standing army now under the United States Government ?

Yes, but it is comparatively a very small one.

How is the law complied with ?

Congress appropriates at one time only enough money to support it for one year.

How might the present army be disbanded ?

Simply by Congress failing to make the necessary appropriation.

How does the system under the Constitution differ from that under the Confederation and the Continental Congress ?

In the old way the Congress declared war, but it was the duty of the States to raise the armies.

How did this system work ?

Very badly indeed; delays and disorders were occasioned by it that prolonged the War of Independence and almost led to the ultimate and utter defeat of the patriots.

What is an army ?

A body of men organized to carry on warfare.

And what is a navy ?

The portion of this body whose operations are conducted at sea.

What nations need a navy ?

Those that have a sea-coast and sea-ports to defend.

Repeat the clauses of Section 8 that refer to warfare.

"The Congress shall have power to declare war, grant letters of marque and reprisal, and make rules concerning captures on land and

water; to raise and support armies; but no
appropriation of money to that use shall be
for a longer term than two years; to provide
and maintain a navy; to make rules for the
government and regulation of the land and
naval forces."

*What forces are at the disposal of Congress besides
the army and navy referred to above?*

The militia of the various States.

How is this power defined?

"The Congress shall have power to provide for
calling forth the militia to execute the laws
of the Union, suppress insurrections, and re-
pel invasions."

*For what purposes, then, may Congress call out the
militia?*

To enforce laws of the United States, to suppress
insurrections anywhere within the territory of the
Union, and to ward off foreign invasions.

Why is this power granted?

Because it may in certain emergencies be necessary
for the maintenance of the public peace.

What evil does it prevent?

The support and menace of a standing army.

Is Congress limited in this power?

No, neither as to time of service nor place of operation.

*Does this power extend beyond the time when Con-
gress is in session?*

Yes, Congress may direct the President to exercise
the same power during a recess, should the exigency
require it.

*What power over the militia is reserved to the
States?*

The appointment of the officers and the authority of training the militia.

Is there any restriction as to this training ?

Yes, the discipline must be such as is prescribed by Congress.

What else is left for Congress to do in the matter ?

To provide not only for organizing, but also for arming and disciplining, the militia, and for governing such part of them as may be employed in the service of the United States.

Why is Congress given this power ?

In order that uniformity may be secured in such particulars as it is deemed necessary.

And why are the States given the training of the militia ?

Because this force is organized mainly for the benefit of the respective States.

CHAPTER XIX.

TERRITORY BELONGING TO THE UNITED STATES.

Over what territory or territories does Congress exercise exclusive control ?

Over the seat of the Federal Government, and over forts, magazines, arsenals, dock-yards, and other such needed places.

How did the Federal Government secure its present seat ?

By cession to it of the territory by the State of Maryland.

What was this territory then called ?
The District of Columbia.
And the city that it was necessary to build there ?
Washington, in honor of the first President.
Was this its first seat ?
No, this territory was not given for some time after the meeting of the First Congress.
Was it the first place suggested for such purpose ?
No; various other places were urged by members of Congress.
Could the Congress accept any extent of territory for this purpose ?
No, such territory was not to exceed ten miles square.
Was the State giving it to retain any authority over it ?
None whatever; it was to surrender all its rights and titles.
What are the words of the clause of the Constitution making these regulations ?

" The Congress shall have power to exercise exclusive legislation, in all cases whatsoever, over such district (not exceeding ten miles square) as may, by cession of particular States, and the acceptance of Congress, become the seat of the Government of the United States."

Who had owned the land on which the City of Washington now stands ?
Daniel Carroll, of Duddington, Maryland's Catholic member of the Constitutional Convention.
May the Congress force a State to sell to it lands for forts, dock-yards, etc. ?
No; it can take such lands only with the consent of the State of which they have formed a part.

What authority has Congress over such lands duly acquired ?

The same that it has over the District of Columbia.

Where do we find the words relating to this matter ?

In the latter part of Clause 16, following those given above.

Repeat them. ·

The Congress shall have power "to exercise like authority over all places purchased, by the consent of the legislature of the State in which the same shall be, for the erection of forts, magazines, arsenals, dock-yards, and other needful buildings."

CHAPTER XX.

POWERS GRANTED AND DENIED TO CONGRESS— SLAVERY.

How does the closing clause of this eighth section of Article I. read ?

"The Congress shall have power to make all laws which shall be necessary and proper for carrying into execution the foregoing powers, and all other powers vested by this Constitution in the Government of the United States, or in any department or officer thereof."

What is the meaning of this clause ?

It is simply declaratory of the powers of Congress not only in reference to the provisions of this section, but also all other matters connected with the Government that require legislation.

Even in this respect does Congress under the Constitution resemble the Congress that preceded it?

No, there is a wide difference between them; the Continental Congress and that of the Confederation could exercise no powers but those mentioned by name and expressly granted by the Articles.

Are any powers denied to Congress by the Constitution?

Yes, Congress is restricted on several points.

What seems to have been the purpose of this restriction?

To preserve the greater freedom and liberty to the citizen.

Where do we find these restrictions?

In the ninth section of Article I.

To what does the first clause of this section refer?

To the importation of certain persons, who are interpreted to mean slaves.

How was slavery to be checked?

By preventing the importation of any more slaves.

Was this to be done at once?

No, not until the year 1808. Congress was in this respect restricted.

Could not Congress interfere at all with the slave trade?

Yes, it might impose the payment of a tax for each slave imported before that date.

Was it restricted in the amount of the tax to be imposed?

Yes; to not more than ten dollars for each person.

Have we any evidence, direct or indirect, that this clause refers to the slave trade?

Yes; in the year 1807 Congress passed a law forbidding the importation of slaves into any State of the Union after January 1, 1808.

In what other part of the world was the importation of slaves prohibited in the same year ?

In the British colonies.

Was such a restriction made in the British colonies before the American Revolution ?

Yes, in several of them; but it was overruled by the crown.

In what States did slavery exist at the time of the adoption of the Constitution ?

In Maryland, Delaware, Virginia, North Carolina, South Carolina, and Georgia.

Had it been extended to any other before the year 1808 ?

Yes, to those formed out of territory that had belonged to these States.

What were they ?

Kentucky, out of part of Virginia, and Tennessee, out of part of North Carolina.

When was slavery entirely abolished in the United States ?

In 1863, during our Civil War.

How was it done ?

By a proclamation of President Lincoln, which was subsequently confirmed by an amendment to the Constitution.

Repeat the clause bearing on the importation of slaves ?

"The migration or importation of such persons as any of the States now existing shall think proper to admit, shall not be prohibited by the Congress prior to the year one thousand eight hundred and eight, but a tax or duty may be imposed on such importation, not exceeding ten dollars for each person."

CHAPTER XXI.

HABEAS CORPUS, JURY TRIAL, ATTAINDER, ETC.

What is the second restriction on Congress ?
It cannot suspend the *habeas corpus* privilege,
unless the public safety be actually in danger.
What do the words "habeas corpus" mean literally ?
" That you have the body."
What is their legal signification ?
That any person taken into custody or imprison-
ment has the right to demand that he be brought
into open court for the purpose of having the cause
of his arrest investigated.
In what part of the proceedings do the words occur ?
In the order of the judge to the official having the
prisoner in custody.
When may the habeas corpus privilege be suspended ?
When the public safety may require it on account
of rebellion or foreign invasion.
In whom is this power of suspension vested ?
In the Congress.
Can the President legally exercise it ?
Not unless it is duly delegated to him by Congress.
Has it ever been exercised by the President ?
Yes, during the Civil War, and without waiting for
the authorization of Congress.
Repeat the clause referring to the habeas corpus writ.
" The privilege of the writ of *habeas corpus*
shall not be suspended, unless when in cases
of rebellion or invasion the public safety
may require it."

What is the inalienable right of every American citizen ?

Trial by jury.

What form of procedure in England, the direct contrary of this trial, was often resorted to ?

Condemnation by act or bill of attainder.

What is an attainder ?

A condemnation, by legislative enactment or judicial discretion, without submitting the case to a jury.

What penalty did it bring ?

It *attainted* the blood of the culprit, entailing the loss of civil rights or estate.

On account of what crimes was it resorted to ?

Treason or other capital offence.

Is it known to our law ?

No; the Constitution forbids it.

What other kindred legislation is also forbidden ?

The making of *ex post facto* laws.

What is an "ex post facto" law ?

A law applying to a deed perpetrated before the law was enacted.

What is it tantamount to ?

Making that a crime which was not a crime when it was done.

Can Congress do such a thing ?

No, it is strictly forbidden to do so.

Repeat the clause referring to the two prohibitions last named ?

> "No bill of attainder, or *ex post facto* law, shall be passed."

CHAPTER XXII.

TAXATION, COMMERCE, AND THE PUBLIC TREASURY.

What is forbidden in regard to the levying of taxes?

That "no capitation or other direct tax shall be laid, unless in proportion to the census or enumeration hereinbefore directed to be taken."

What is the meaning of this clause?

That if a tax be levied at all, it must be levied equally on all sections of the country, in proportion to the population.

Are duties on exports permitted?

No; it is laid down that "no tax or duty shall be laid on articles exported from any State."

To what may these words refer besides goods sent out of the country?

To commerce between the States themselves.

What would be its bearing in this case?

The prevention of discrimination in trade against any State or States.

Is this equality of the States more explicitly set forth in this part of the Constitution?

Yes, in the words that follow those quoted above, which are:

"No preference shall be given by any regulation of commerce or revenue to the ports of one State over those of another; nor shall vessels bound to or from one State be obliged to enter, clear, or pay duties in another."

What is the full meaning of these words?
That there shall ever be entire freedom of commerce between the States.

Does any advantage accrue from not levying duties on exports?
Yes, our products which are not needed for consumption at home are thus given a better chance in foreign markets.

How did Great Britain restrain the commerce of her colonies?
By compelling vessels from the colonies to go by way of England to any part of the world, even those bound from one American colony to another.

Can Congress thus direct commerce to any particular port or section?
No; the Constitution prohibits it.

Under what restriction is the Government placed in regard to public moneys?
No money can be drawn from the Treasury without the warranty of special legal enactment of Congress.

How is this regulated?
Congress must pass a law specifying the appropriations to be made.

Must an account be kept of all moneys thus appropriated?
"A regular statement and account of the receipts and expenditures of all public money" shall not only be kept, but also "be published from time to time."

Is this a wise regulation?
Yes, it makes both Congress and the Executive directly responsible to the people for all moneys passing out of the Treasury.

CHAPTER XXIII.

TITLES OF NOBILITY AND HONORS.

Are titles of nobility permitted under the United States Government?

No; our Government is expressly forbidden to grant them.

Is this a commendable provision?

Yes, for it preserves the principle of equality among our citizens, no matter how pre-eminent may be the abilities or services of some of them.

Are Americans restrained from accepting honors, presents, and titles from foreign potentates and powers?

Only such persons as hold offices of profit or trust under the United States are so restrained.

Can these not accept under any circumstances?

Yes, they can, by the special consent of Congress.

What principle would seem to have prompted this regulation?

The fear that such officers might thus be amenable to foreign influence.

How does this last clause of Section 9 read?

"No title of nobility shall be granted by the United States, and no person holding any office of profit or trust under them shall, without the consent of the Congress, accept of any present, emolument, office, or title of any kind whatever, from any king, prince, or foreign state."

CHAPTER XXIV.

POWERS DENIED TO THE STATES.

Are any powers forbidden to the States individually?
Yes, all those reserved solely to the Federal Government or that would conflict with its authority, as well as those powers that are denied to Congress.

How are they enumerated?
As follows, in the first clause of Section 10 of Article I., which says:

> "No State shall enter into any treaty, alliance, or confederation; grant letters of marque and reprisal; coin money; emit bills of credit; make anything but gold and silver coin a tender for payment of debts; pass any bill of attainder, *ex post facto* law, or law impairing the obligation of contracts; or grant any title of nobility."

Why is it not necessary to consider most of these restrictions here?
Because they have been dealt with already in considering the restrictions of the Federal or General Government.

Why are they laid down so plainly?
In order to prevent any conflict of authority between a State and the General Government.

Why should a State of the Union not have the power to grant letters of marque and reprisal?
Because thus a small number of the body politic could at any time involve the whole country in war.

Why is the coining of money forbidden to the States?

Because too great a variety of currency, both as to denomination and to value, might thus be introduced.

What are bills of credit?

Promises to pay money that are put in the form of a circulating medium.

Did the States at any time thus make use of them?

Yes, during the Revolutionary War and the time of the Confederation.

By what name were they then known?

As Continental money.

Was their success encouraging?

No; it was so far from being so that it was no wonder a clause against them was introduced into the Constitution.

Is a State, then, forbidden to borrow money on bonds?

No; but in redeeming these bonds it must pay its obligations in gold and silver coin.

To what does the other clause of this tenth section refer?

To powers which the States can exercise only under the sanction of Congress.

Name one of these.

A State can, for instance, with the consent of Congress, lay such imposts or duties as are absolutely necessary for executing its inspection laws.

What power has Congress over such laws?

That of revision.

In case there is an excess of such imposts over what is needed by the State, what is done with it?

It is turned into the Treasury of the United States.

What is an inspection law?

An enactment requiring the careful examination

and approval of certain commodities before they are exported.

Repeat that part of the clause referring to inspection laws and imposts?

"No State shall, without the consent of the Congress, lay any imposts or duties on imports or exports, except what may be absolutely necessary for executing its inspection laws; and the net produce of all duties and imposts laid by any State on imports or exports shall be for the use of .the Treasury of the United States, and all such laws shall be subject to the revision and control of Congress."

What is the next regulation laid down in this clause?

That no State shall, without the consent of Congress, lay any duty of tonnage.

How might a State endanger the public peace and safety?

By keeping troops or ships of war in time of peace.

Is she, then, forbidden to keep these?

Yes, for the better preservation of the public peace.

How else might the safety of the Union be endangered by the States?

By allowing them to enter into any agreement or compact with another State, or with a foreign power, or engage in war.

These things are forbidden to the States, then?

Yes, under ordinary circumstances.

Why do you say "under ordinary circumstances"?

Because it may become necessary for a State to engage in war on account of being actually invaded or in such imminent danger as will not admit of delay.

Is this exception specified in the Constitution?

It is so specified, clearly and very explicitly.

CHAPTER XXV.

THE EXECUTIVE POWER.

If Congress is the power that makes the law, what is the power that carries the law into execution ?

The Executive Power.

In whom does the Constitution vest the executive power ?

In a President.

Where do we find this provision in the Constitution ?

In the first clause of the first section of Article II.

Repeat the words.

" The executive power shall be vested in a President of the United States of America."

What other provision is made in the same clause ?

The length of the term for which the President shall hold his office.

How long is this term ?

Four years.

What other officer is elected at the same time, in the same manner, and for the same term ?

The Vice-President.

Repeat the words of Clause 1 bearing on these two officers.

" He (the President) shall hold his office during the term of four years, and, together with the Vice-President, be elected," etc.

Does the President actually perform all the duties of the executive branch of government himself ?

No ; most of these duties are performed by various corps of officials divided into separate departments, whose heads are directly responsible to him.

Why was this arrangement adopted ?

Because good policy demands that the government should be organized in the mode best calculated to attain with precision and fidelity the execution of the law.

How many departments are thus organized under the executive branch of the government of the United States ?

Eight, namely: the departments of State, of the Treasury, of Justice, of the Post-Office, of War, of the Navy, of the Interior, and of Agriculture.

Were all these departments organized at the beginning of our government ?

No, only the five first named.

When were the others added ?

That of the Navy in 1798, that of the Interior in 1849, and that of Agriculture as late as the year 1889.

How were they added ?

By Act of Congress.

What are the duties of the Department of the Interior ?

It has a general authority of supervision and appeal over the subjects of patents, public lands and mines, Indian affairs, pensions, public buildings, the accounts of marshals, clerks, and public officers, as well as over other minor subjects.

Why have Catholics often had occasion to find fault with the management of this department ?

Because of gross injustice done to Catholic missionaries among the Indians, and to Indian tribes converted to Catholicity.

What is the title of the head of each department ?

The Secretary of such department, except in the cases of those of Justice and of the Post-Office.

How is the former styled ?

The Attorney-General of the United States.

And the latter ?

As Postmaster-General.

By what other title is the head of a department known ?

By that of a Cabinet officer.

Why does he get this title ?

Because by his office he is a member of the President's Cabinet, or board of advisers.

Who takes precedence, or the first place, in the Cabinet ?

The Secretary of State.

What is his principal duty ?

To look after the relations of the United States with foreign countries.

How are these Cabinet officers chosen ?

By the President himself, subject, however, to the approval of the Senate.

Must he also ask the Senate's permission to get rid of them ?

No ; he can dismiss them of his own accord.

CHAPTER XXVI.

ELECTION OF THE PRESIDENT.

How is the President himself chosen ?
By delegates representing the various States.
He is not, then, elected directly by the people ?
No, but by the States in their capacity as individual commonwealths.
By what name are the State delegates chosen to elect a President known ?
By that of electors.
How are they chosen ?
By a plurality of the popular vote of each State.
How many electors may each State choose ?
As many as it has Senators and Representatives in Congress.
How many do these number at present ?
They number 401.
How many electoral votes are necessary to elect the President ?
A majority of this number, or 201.
May any citizen serve as an elector ?
No ; certain citizens are disqualified from serving as electors.
Who are they ?
Senators and Representatives in Congress, and all persons holding offices of trust or profit under the United States Government.
Where are these regulations laid down ?
In Clause 2 of the first section of Article II.
What are the words of this clause ?
"Each State shall appoint, in such manner as

the legislature thereof may direct, a number of electors equal to the whole number of Senators and Representatives to which the State may be entitled in the Congress; but no Senator or Representative, or person holding an office of trust or profit under the United States, shall be appointed an elector."

Are all the details of the election of a President the same now that they were when the Constitution went first into effect?

No; some important matters of detail have been materially changed.

How were these changes authorized?

By the adoption in due form of an amendment to the Constitution.

Where were the original regulations laid down?

In the third clause of Section 1 of Article II

Is the whole of this clause now of no effect?

Yes; it has been annulled or repealed.

And by what measure are the new rules laid down?

By Article XII. of the Amendments to the Constitution.

When was this amendment adopted?

During the first session of the Eighth Congress.

What is the first important change which this amendment has made?

Originally in each State the electors had to vote for two candidates for President, and they did not vote at all expressly for a Vice-President.

And what is the rule now?

They have to cast two separate sets of ballots, which have to be kept distinct from each other: one for President and one for Vice-President.

And how, then, was the Vice-President chosen in the beginning ?

The candidate for President who had received the second highest number of votes was declared to have been elected Vice-President.

Was any restriction laid down as to the two persons to be voted for ?

Yes; they could not be inhabitants of the same State.

Have we in the new law an equivalent of this restriction ?

We have; the candidates for President and Vice-President must belong to different States.

How did the restriction read in the old law ?

"The electors shall meet in their respective States and vote by ballot for *two persons, one of whom at least shall not be an inhabitant of the same State with themselves.*"

And in the new ?

"The electors shall meet in their respective States and vote by ballot for *President and Vice-President, one of whom at least,*" etc.

What further rule and precaution is laid down in the new law ?

That the electors "shall name, in their ballots, the person voted for as President, and in distinct ballots the person voted for as Vice-President."

And as to recording the ballots and the names of the candidates voted for, what was the original regulation ?

It was thus laid down: "They shall make *a list* of all the persons voted for, and of the number of votes for each."

And in the new ?

"They shall make *distinct lists* of all persons

voted for as President, and of all persons voted for as Vice-President, and of the number of votes for each."

What is then done with these lists?

They are signed and certified to, and then carefully sealed and transmitted to the seat of government of the United States.

Was the process different of old?

No, except that only one list was made out.

To whom is the sealed package directed?

To the President of the Senate.

How many such packages does he receive?

As many as there are States of the Union.

And what is the President of the Senate to do with them?

He, in the presence of the members of both the Senate and the House of Representatives, opens all the certificates, and then and there the votes are counted.

How is the result announced?

The person receiving the highest number of votes cast for President, if that number be a majority of all the electors appointed, is declared to have been duly elected President.

And if the highest number be not a majority of all the electors, then what is done?

The decision is referred to the House of Representatives, which is required to act immediately.

How does the House elect the President?

Each State casts one ballot.

How is it decided that the ballot shall be cast?

By vote of the majority of the members of the House of Representatives from that State.

What is then necessary to a choice?

Delegates from at least two-thirds of the States must be present, and the successful candidate must receive a majority of votes of all the States.

Is the House restricted as to the candidates from among whom the President shall be chosen ?

Yes; it is limited to those voted for by the electors.

May all these be voted for ?

No; not more than three of them.

And how are these determined ?

They must be those having received the highest numbers respectively of electoral votes.

What strange anomaly might have arisen in the old system of choosing the President ?

Two candidates might receive the same number of votes and both have a majority.

What course was to be taken in that case ?

The election was to be referred to the House of Representatives, where one of the two was to be chosen.

And if no candidate had a majority, then what was done ?

From the five highest on the list the said House was to choose the President, the votes being taken by States, as now.

Before what date must the election have been completed ?

Before the 4th of March of every fourth year.

Why then ?

Because the Presidential term begins on that day.

How is it arranged that the process may be completed then ?

The dates are fixed on which the electors shall act in the separate States, before which the certificates shall reach the seat of government, and on which the votes shall be counted by the President of the Senate.

CHAPTER XXVII.

THE VICE-PRESIDENT.

When the election is thrown into the House and the House fails to act before the 4th of March, what is to be done?

The Vice-President will then assume the duties of President.

In what other cases may the Vice-President act thus?

In case of the death or other constitutional disability of the President.

How is the Vice-President elected?

In the same manner as the President, except when a clear majority of the whole number of electors may fail to vote for the same man.

And if no person have such a majority, how is the office filled?

Then from the two names on the list receiving the highest number of votes the Vice-President shall be chosen by the Senate.

How many Senators must be present for this purpose?

Two-thirds of the whole number.

How many votes are necessary for a choice?

A majority of the whole number.

Do they vote by States?

Not necessarily, but practically they do, as all the States are equally represented in the Senate.

How does this law differ from the old one?

In the old system, in every case, after the choice of the President the person having the greatest number of votes of the electors became the Vice-President.

If two candidates had each received the next highest number of votes, what was done?

CATECHISM OF THE CONSTITUTION.

Then the Senate chose the Vice-President from among them by ballot.

What qualifications are required in the Vice-President?

The same as in the President, which will be discussed later on.

And why is this?

Because in certain emergencies the Vice-President may be called upon to assume the duties of President.

While the President remains in office, what is the principal duty of the Vice-President?

To preside over the deliberations of the Senate.

Can he vote in that body?

Not unless there be an even division, or a tie vote, as it is popularly called.

In whom is vested the power of determining the time for choosing the electors?

In Congress.

Has it any other power in regard to them?

Yes; it is empowered also to name the day on which they shall give their votes.

How is it limited in the appointment of these days?

The day for the performance of each duty must be the same throughout the United States.

What is the day popularly called on which the electors are chosen?

That of the Presidential election.

On what day is this election held?

On the Tuesday next following the first Monday of November of every fourth year.

Has this always been the day?

No.

How and when was this date decided on?

By act of Congress of January 23, 1845.

CHAPTER XXVIII.

ELIGIBILITY TO THE PRESIDENCY.

Who are eligible for the office of President?
All citizens born within the limits of the United
States who have attained the age of thirty-five years.
Did this restriction always prevail?
No.
Who besides were eligible formerly?
All who had been citizens when the Constitution
was adopted and who had been residents of the
country fourteen years before coming up for election.
*Of what importance, then, is the doubt about the
birthplace of Andrew Jackson?*
None whatever; it makes no difference whether he
was born in South Carolina, or on the ocean, or in
Carrickfergus, Ireland.
*What are the words of the clause of the Constitution
bearing on this point?*

> " No person except a natural-born citizen, or
> a *citizen of the United States at the time of
> the adoption of this Constitution,* shall be
> eligible for the office of President; neither
> shall any person be eligible to that office
> who shall not have attained to the age of
> thirty-five years, and been *fourteen years a
> resident within the United States.*"

*When did the words italicized in the preceding
sentence become inoperative?*
When all those were dead who had been citizens at
the time of the adoption of the Constitution.

Who of those residing abroad can still be elected to the Presidency ?

Such as are engaged in the public service of the United States.

When may the Vice-President become the acting President of the United States ?

When the President is removed from office, or dies, or resigns, or becomes unfit to discharge the powers and duties of his office.

And what is done in case both the President and the Vice-President should be removed, die, resign, or become incapacitated ?

Congress may provide for such an emergency by enacting a succession law, declaring what officer shall then act as President.

Has such an enactment ever been made ?

Yes; a Presidential succession act was passed as late as 1887.

To whom is the succession given in this act ?

To the Secretary of State under the late President.

How long may he act ?

Until the disability be removed or a new Presidential election be held.

CHAPTER XXIX.

COMPENSATION AND PRIVILEGES OF THE PRESIDENT.

What compensation may the President receive on account of his office ?

Such an annual sum as the Congress may deem fit.

What salary does the President now receive ?

A yearly allowance of fifty thousand dollars.

Was it always so much ?

No; it was only half of this sum before the beginning of General Grant's second term in office.

What restriction is laid down as to the salary ?

That it shall neither be increased nor diminished during any one Presidential term.

Is this a wise provision ?

Yes, for otherwise a President might abuse his personal and official interest and influence to have it increased, or Congress might diminish it to annoy a President not in harmony with their views.

In what other respect as to worldly gain is the President restricted ?

During his term of office he can receive no emolument but his salary from either the United States or any of the States. ▸

Repeat the words of the clause in reference to the compensation of the President.

> " The President shall, at stated times, receive for his services a compensation which shall neither be increased nor diminished during the period for which he shall have been elected, and he shall not receive within that

period any other emolument from the United States, or any of them."

What must the President do before entering on the duties or execution of his office ?

He must take an oath or affirmation.

Are the words of this oath prescribed in the Constitution ?

They are.

Repeat them.

" I do solemnly swear (or affirm) that I will faithfully execute the office of President of the United States, and will, to the best of my ability, preserve, protect, and defend the Constitution of the United States."

What other office does the President hold by virtue of his office as President ?

That of Commander-in-Chief of the Army and Navy of the United States and of the militia of the several States when called into the service of the United States.

Who is commander of the State Militia at other times ?

The Governor of each State.

Why was the President entrusted with this power ?

To make the military force more easily and effectively available for service in case of danger.

Does the President call these forces into action ?

No ; this is the duty of Congress ; he only assumes command of them in the field.

What power has he over the executive departments ?

He may demand the opinion, in writing, of the principal officer in each of them, on subjects relating to the duties of the Cabinet officers.

Has he any pardoning power ?

Yes; he has power to grant reprieves and pardons for offences against the United States.

For all such offences without exception ?

. No; cases of impeachment are excepted.

Why ?

Because as such they entail only removal from office.

What power has he to treat with foreign nations ?

That of making treaties with them.

Absolutely ?

No; only by and with the advice and consent of the Senate.

What is the character of this consent ?

Two-thirds of the Senators taking part in the affair must concur.

In what other important matter must the Senate similarly concur with him ?

In the matter of appointments to important offices.

What officers may he thus nominate ?

Ambassadors and ministers to foreign courts, consuls at various trading points, judges of the Supreme and other courts of the United States, and, in fact, all United States officials not otherwise provided for and which shall be established by.law.

Can Congress limit this power of the President ?

It may by law invest the appointment of inferior officers in the courts of law, or in the heads of departments.

And may Congress increase the President's power ?

Yes; it can also vest such appointments in him alone.

Can the President make appointments without the concurrence of the Senate ?

He can at certain times only.

When may he do this ?

During a recess of Congress.

How does he do so ?

By granting commissions.

How long will these commissions hold good ?

Only until the end of the next session of the Senate.

Why is such provision made ?

Because during a recess vacancies may occur by death or from other causes.

Is the concurrence of the Senate necessary in cases of removal from office by the President ?

No.

Is there a constitutional provision to this effect ?

No; it is simply an immemorial custom.

What other direct relations may the President have with the Congress ?

He is required to give, from time to time, information of the state of the Union, and to recommend to the consideration of Congress such measures as he shall judge necessary and expedient.

Has he any control over the time and length of the sessions of Congress ?

Yes; he may, on extraordinary occasions, convene both Houses, or either of them.

By what name are such sessions called ?

By that of extra, or extraordinary, sessions.

Why are they so called ?

To distinguish them from the regular session, which begins each year on the first Monday of December.

Has he any other power over the sessions of Congress ?

Yes; in case of disagreement between the two Houses with respect to the time of adjournment he may adjourn them.

For how long a period may this adjournment last ?

Until such time as he shall think proper.

How does he stand with regard to envoys from foreign countries ?

It is his special province and duty to receive all ambassadors and other public ministers.

What supervisory power is the President entrusted with as regards the laws in general ?

He is instructed to take care that the laws be faithfully carried into effect.

What is necessary for all officers of the United States before they can enter upon the duties of their respective offices ?

They must be furnished with a commission from the President.

Is this important ?

Yes ; they should be able to produce proper credentials.

What is an impeachment ?

An accusation and prosecution for treason or other high crimes or misdemeanors.

May the President of the United States be impeached?

He may.

For what cause or causes ?

For treason, bribery, or other high crimes.

What is the penalty of conviction ?

Removal from office and disqualification from holding office thereafter.

May others than the President be impeached ?

Yes; the Vice-President and, in fact, all *civil* officers of the United States.

CHAPTER XXX.

THE JUDICIARY.

What is the third department of the government of the United States ?
The Judiciary or judicial department.
What is its chief function ?
The administration of justice.
Why is this branch of our political system of the greatest interest to us ?
Because it interferes more visibly and uniformly than any other with the concerns of life.
How does this happen ?
By the fact that it deals directly with the rights of personal security and private property.
Is it important, then, to have none but upright men in the judiciary ?
Most important, because these rights rest entirely on the wisdom, the stability, and the integrity of the courts of justice.
What is the first principle regarding them laid down in the Constitution ?
It declares that " the judicial power of the United States shall be vested in one Supreme Court, and in such inferior courts as the Congress may from time to time ordain and establish."
Is Congress at liberty to establish such courts or not ?
No ; the Constitution is mandatory upon the legislature to establish courts of justice commensurate with the judicial power and needs of the Union.

How does the judicial power compare in point of authority with the other powers of the Government ?

It is equal with them, and this power is as exclusively vested in the proper courts as is the legislative power in Congress, or the executive power in the President.

What courts does the Constitution order to be created ?

A Supreme Court and whatever inferior courts may be deemed necessary.

By what name are those called who are appointed to administer justice in these courts ?

They are called justices or judges.

How long shall they hold their offices ?

As long as they behave themselves in a becoming manner.

How are they constituted ?

They are nominated or appointed by the President.

Has he absolute control over their appointment ?

No; we have already seen that these appointments are made by and with the advice and consent of the Senate.

By whom is the first step taken in these appointments ?

By the President, who submits names of candidates to the Senate.

And what is the duty of the Senate in this case ?

Either to approve or reject the nominations.

What is necessary for approval ?

A majority vote.

What courts has the Congress power to constitute at pleasure ?

Such inferior to the Supreme Court as may be

deemed necessary for transacting the legal business of the United States.

How many classes of these courts have so far been constituted?

Two; namely, Circuit and District Courts.

Which of these has the higher and wider jurisdiction?

The Circuit Courts, which are the more closely connected with the Supreme Court.

How many Circuit Courts are there?

Nine, or one for each Supreme Court judge.

And how many District Courts?

Forty-two.

How long do the judges of these courts hold their office?

During good behavior, the same as the judges of the Supreme Court.

And how may they be removed from office?

By impeachment for misconduct.

How are they remunerated for their services?

They receive such salaries as the Congress may deem competent.

What is laid down regarding this salary?

That it shall not be diminished during their continuance in office.

Why is this considered a wise provision?

Because through it the judges are secured from intimidation by Congress.

Is the method of choosing the judges likewise based on wisdom?

Yes; for the fewer and higher in authority are those to whom they owe their office, the more likely is it that their decisions will not be influenced by popular passion or prejudice.

Repeat the words of the Constitution bearing on the tenure of office and salary of United States court judges.

"The judges, both of the Supreme and inferior courts, shall hold their offices during good behavior; and shall, at stated times, receive for their services a compensation which shall not be diminished during their continuance in office."

CHAPTER XXXI.

JURISDICTION OF THE UNITED STATES COURTS.

How far does the judicial power of the United States extend?

To all cases in law and equity arising under the Constitution, the laws and treaties of the Union, and appertaining to all the services of the United States, as well as to cases arising between the Union and the separate States and between this country and foreign countries, between States of the Union, and between a State and the citizens of another State.

How far should the judicial power extend?

It should be co-extensive with the power of legislation in the same political system.

How does it stand accordingly in our system?

It is the final expositor of the Constitution as to all questions of a judicial nature.

How does the Constitution define the cases over which the judicial power has control?

It states them in classes so clearly that there can be no mistake about them.

What cases belong to the first class ?

"All cases, in law and equity, arising under this Constitution, the laws of the United States, and treaties made, or which shall be made, under their authority."

What cases belong to the second class of those brought before the United States courts ?

"All cases affecting ambassadors, other public ministers and consuls."

Are these officers amenable to any other law than that of the State which they are serving ?

Yes; to the law of nations.

Why ?

Because they are engaged in international affairs.

Why are they not amenable to the laws of the country to which they are sent ?

Because they hold the place of the State sending them, which acknowledges no subjection to any other State.

What cases are laid down in the next class as belonging to the United States courts ?

"All cases of admiralty and maritime jurisdiction."

Why are these cases brought before the courts of the United States ?

Because, as we have seen, the United States Government has control over commerce in all the navigable waters of the country and over happenings on the high seas.

What is the next class of cases ?

"Controversies to which the United States shall be a party."

Why is this provision made ?
Because, obviously, the United States should not
be compelled to have recourse to the courts of any
one of the States.

Why not ?
For the reason that a superior power should not
have to appeal to an inferior power for settlement of
a dispute.

What cases are contained in the last class ?
> "Controversies between two or more States,
> between a State and citizens of another
> State, between citizens of different States,
> between citizens of the same State claiming
> lands under grants of different States, and
> between a State, or the citizens thereof, and
> foreign states, citizens, or subjects."

What is peculiar about these cases ?
The parties to them belong to different States, or
claim under laws of different States.

*How many kinds of controversies may arise accord-
ing to this class ?*
Five.

What are those of the first class ?
Those between two or more States.

Of the second ?
Between a State and citizens of another State.

The third ?
Between citizens of different States.

The fourth ?
Between citizens of the same State claiming lands
under grants of different States.

The fifth ?
Between a State, or its citizens, and foreign states,
citizens, or subjects.

Why is it the better part of wisdom in such case to have recourse to the Federal courts ?

Because in the State courts too much partiality might be shown to litigants belonging to the same State as the court.

What, then, would be the result if such cases were left to the State courts ?

Jealousies and animosities between the States themselves, and enmities of these States against foreign countries.

What defect was found in this clause of the Constitution as originally framed ?

It was discovered that any private citizen could bring in the Federal courts suit against a State, even against that of which he himself was a citizen.

Was it thought wise to limit this power of individual private citizens ?

Yes, and even necessary, lest in a very short time more cases would be referred to the Federal courts than they could dispose of in years.

What other complaint was made against this practice ?

That it was derogatory to the dignity of the sovereignty of the State.

What was then done by way of remedying the evil ?

An amendment to the Constitution was proposed and adopted.

When was this done ?

At the second session of the Third Congress.

What are the words of this amendment ?

"The judicial power of the United States shall not be construed to extend to any suit in law or equity commenced or prosecuted against one of the United States by citizens of another State, or by citizens or subjects of any foreign state."

How far does the inhibition apply?

Only to citizens or subjects, and does not extend to suits by a State or by foreign states or powers.

CHAPTER XXXII.

JURISDICTION AND ORGANIZATION OF THE SUPREME COURT.

In what cases has the Supreme Court original jurisdiction?

"In all cases affecting ambassadors, other public ministers and consuls, and those in which a State shall be a party."

What other kind of jurisdiction is the Supreme Court said to have?

Appellate jurisdiction.

When may it exercise this?

In all other cases than those named above.

Without any exception?

No; with such exceptions and under such regulations as the Congress shall make.

Can you state the distinction between original and appellate jurisdiction?

The former refers to cases that have been before no other court, the latter to those brought up from another and lower court.

By what power is the Supreme Court constituted?

By the Constitution, as we have seen already.

Did the Constitution also provide for the details of its organization ?

No; this it has received from Congress.

Of whom does it consist ?

Of nine judges.

Are they all equal in rank and title ?

No ; one of them is superior to the others.

How is he distinguished ?

By being called the Chief-Justice.

How are the others styled ?

Associate Justices.

When the Chief-Justiceship becomes vacant, is one of the Associate Justices promoted to the vacant place ?

No, though the law does not forbid this being done.

Why has such a promotion not been regarded with favor ?

Because it was thought that such promotion might lead to unseemly rivalries among the associate judges.

How many Chief-Justices have sat on the Supreme bench ?

Eight; namely, John Jay, John Rutledge, Oliver Ellsworth, John Marshall, Roger B. Taney, Salmon P. Chase, Morrison R. Waite, and Melville W. Fuller.

Who are the two best known of these ?

John Marshall and Roger B. Taney.

Besides being the ablest jurists, what else was remarkable about them ?

Their terms of office were the longest.

Why should Catholics take especial pride in remembering Chief-Justice Taney ?

Because he was the most eminent Catholic civilian of this country.

How many of the judges constitute a quorum ?
Five.
Did the Court always consist of nine judges ?
No; originally there were but six, which number
was increased to seven in 1807, to nine in 1837, to ten
in 1863; decreased to nine in 1865, to eight in 1867,
and again increased to nine in 1870.

*What is the 'salary of a Judge of the Supreme
Court ?*
Ten thousand dollars for each of the Associate Jus-
tices, and ten thousand five hundred for the Chief-
Justice.

How many terms does the court hold annually ?
Only one.

When is this term begun ?
On the first Monday in December.

How long does it last ?
As long as the court itself may see fit.

Where is it held ?
At the seat of Government, in Washington.

*State the jurisdiction of the Supreme Court with
regard to the States.*

"The Supreme Court," says Kent, "has exclusive jurisdiction of all controversies of a civil
nature, where a State is a party, except between a State as *defendant* and its citizens;
and except, also, between a State as *defendant* and citizens of other States, or aliens, in
which case it has no jurisdiction; but in all
these cases where a State is *plaintiff* it has
original, but not exclusive, jurisdiction."

CHAPTER XXXIII.

THE CIRCUIT AND DISTRICT COURTS.

From what courts may appeals be made to the Supreme Court?

From the Circuit and District Courts and from the courts of the several States.

In all cases?

No; only in civil actions and suits in equity.

Why are the Circuit Courts so called?

Because each has charge of one of the circuits into which the whole territory of the United States is divided.

Have these circuits been always the same in number and territory?

No; the limits and jurisdiction of these courts have been subject to occasional changes, and their number has varied, as has the number of justices of the Supreme Court.

With what powers are they vested?

They are vested with original cognizance, concurrent with the courts of the several States, of all suits of a civil nature where the matter in dispute exceeds $500 and the United States is plaintiff, or an alien is a party, and the suit is between a citizen of the State where the suit is brought and a citizen of another State.

Have they any jurisdiction in criminal matters?

They have exclusive cognizance of all crimes and offences cognizable under the authority of the United States, exceeding the degree of ordinary misdemeanors.

And what of these crimes ?

They belong to the jurisdiction of the District Courts as well as of the Circuit Courts.

What rank do the District Courts hold in the judicial system of the United States ?

They are the lowest of the three grades.

What are the limitations of trial as to districts ?

No person can be arrested in one district for trial in another, and no civil suit can be brought against an inhabitant of the United States out of his district.

How is a close connection established between the Circuit Courts and the Supreme Court ?

One of the justices of the latter presides over the deliberations of theformer.

What form of trial in these courts is laid down for crimes ?

The trial by jury.

In all cases ?

No; cases of impeachment are excepted.

By whom are these tried ?

By the United States Senate.

What are the words of the Constitution in this regard ?

" The trial of all crimes, except in cases of impeachment, shall be by jury."

Where is such trial to be held ?

In the State where the crimes to be punished have been committed.

Repeat the exact words as to this provision.

" Such trial shall be held in the State where the said crimes shall have been committed."

What advantages flow from this provision ?

The trial takes place where the facts are best known, the accused has less difficulty in procuring testimony, and is likely to be put to less expense.

But suppose the crime be committed not within the jurisdiction of any State—as, for instance, at sea,— where is the trial to be held ?

In such place as the Congress may direct.

What are the words to this effect ?

"When (the crime is) not committed within any State, the trial shall be at such place, or places, as the Congress may by law have directed."

CHAPTER XXXIV.

TREASON AGAINST THE UNITED STATES.

In what does the crime of treason against the United States consist ?

In levying war against them or in adhering to their enemies.

What is the advantage of having the crime of treason thus clearly defined ?

To prevent, in times of great political excitement, other and less heinous offences from being exaggerated into treason and construed as such.

How may a person be convicted of treason ?

Only on the testimony of two witnesses to the same overt act, or on confession in open court.

What advantage is derived from having two witnesses ?

The accused has thus better protection against misrepresentation.

Why is danger of false accusation feared here more than in other cases ?

Because in a time of great excitement persons may take advantage of public feeling to annoy an enemy or opponent.

Why will not any confession be taken as proof of treason ?

Because it may sometimes be made in an unguarded moment and exaggerated by excitement or surroundings.

What is the advantage of requiring that it be made in open court ?

To insure that it be reported correctly.

Repeat the definition of treason.

" Treason against the United States shall consist only in levying war against them, or in adhering to their enemies, giving them aid and comfort."

And those as to conviction for treason.

" No person shall be convicted of treason, unless on the testimony of two witnesses to the same overt act, or on confession in open court."

How is the punishment for treason regulated ?

By the Congress.

In what respect is it limited in declaring punishment ?

To the effect that a conviction of treason cannot work corruption of blood, or forfeiture of possessions, except during the life of the culprit.

How does our law in this respect differ from that of England ?

In England not only was the traitor put to death in the most cruel and savage manner, but his blood was declared corrupted and all his goods were confiscated for ever.

What is meant by corruption of blood ?
Loss of the power to transmit inheritance.
How long may this disqualification have effect in the United States ?
Only during the life-time of the person attainted of treason.
Repeat the clause bearing on the punishment for treason.
" The Congress shall have power to declare the punishment of treason, but no attainder of treason shall work corruption of blood, or forfeiture, except during the life of the person attainted."

CHAPTER XXXV.

CONCURRENT POWERS OF THE STATES.

Does the Constitution make the acts of one State binding on another ?
It does, in public and legal matters.
What are the words to this effect ?
" Full faith and credit shall be given in each State to the public acts, records, and judicial proceedings of every other State."
Wherein is vested the power of regulating details in this matter ?
In Congress.
Can Congress prescribe anything else in reference thereto ?
Yes, the effect of these proceedings.

What are the words bearing thereon ?
They are these :
> "And the Congress may, by general laws,
> prescribe the manner in which such acts,
> records, and proceedings shall be proved, and
> the effect thereof."

What is the practical outcome of this regulation ?
That a legal decision in one State is of binding
force in another.

Of what benefit is this ?
It is not necessary to repeat the same proceedings
in every State in which the parties may have interests.

*In what respects do the States possess concurrent
powers ?*
In both legislative and judicial matters.

*May State courts take cognizance of cases arising
under the Constitution of the United States ?*
They may, subject to revision by the United States
Supreme Court, by means of its appellate jurisdiction.

Are the rights of citizenship the same in all the States ?
The Constitution makes such a guarantee.

Have all citizens the same privileges in all the States?
No ; in some they have more, in some less.

Can you mention any instances ?
Yes, in that of the electoral franchise particularly,
wherein there has been great variation, as we have
seen.

*Does the spirit of the Constitution, then, seem to have
been disregarded ?*
Yes, as its words read.

Repeat these words.
> "The citizens of each State shall be entitled to
> all privileges and immunities of citizens in
> the several States."

Can one State protect criminals fleeing from another State ?

No; all refugees from justice on account of crime must be given up to the authorities of the State in which the crime has been committed.

What is the method of procedure in this case ?

The executive authority of the State in which the crime has been committed issues a requisition on the executive authority of the State in which the criminal has taken refuge.

What is then done ?

The criminal, if in custody, is delivered up to the State issuing the requisition.

Repeat the clause bearing on the restoration of fugitive criminals.

" A person charged in any State with treason, felony, or other crime, who shall flee from justice, and be found in another State, shall, on demand of the executive authority of the State from which he fled, be delivered up, to be removed to the State having jurisdiction of the crime."

What other class of persons were formerly to be delivered up ?

Fugitive slaves, who appear to have been the persons subject to the provisions of Clause 3 of the second section of Article IV. of the Constitution.

Are persons of this class to be returned now ?

No.

Why ?

Because there are no slaves.

Who else might be considered as coming under this clause ?

All persons held to service or labor for a specified time.

Who might they be ?
Principally apprentices.
Repeat the clause referring to runaways.

"No person held to service or labor in one
State under the laws thereof, escaping into
another, shall, in consequence of any law or
regulation therein, be discharged from such
service or labor; but shall be delivered up
on claim of the party to whom such service
or labor may be due."

What subsequent legislation has affected this clause ?
The amendment to the Constitution abolishing
slavery.

CHAPTER XXXVI.

FORMATION OF NEW STATES AND GOVERNMENT OF TERRITORIES.

What is the subject of the third section of Article IV.?
The method of admitting new States into the Union
and the government of Territories of the United
States.

How are new States admitted into the Union ?
By act of Congress.

How are new States formed ?
Out of the Territories of the United States.

*May a State already in the Union be subdivided into
two or more States ?*
Yes.

May this be done by an act of Congress alone ?
No.

What else is required ?
An act of the Legislature of the State to be divided.
Has this law been always strictly observed ?
No; it has once been disregarded.
In what case ?
In that of the separation of West Virginia from Virginia in 1862.
Why was this ?
Because Virginia was then in rebellion against the Union.
In what other way may new States be formed ?
By the union of two or more States or parts of States.
Can this be done merely by act of Congress ?
No; acts of the legislatures of all the States concerned are likewise required.
How many new States have been formed since the adoption of the Constitution ?
Twenty-five.
May other new States be formed ?
Yes; four are now in process of formation, as we have seen.
Have any two States been united into one ?
No.
What are the words of the clause bearing on the formation of new States ?

> ' New States may be admitted by the Congress into this Union, but no new State shall be formed or erected within the jurisdiction of any other State, nor any State be formed by the junction of two or more States, or parts of States, without the consent of the legislatures of the States concerned, as well as of the Congress."

Can you name the States that were not of the original thirteen, and the dates of their admission into the Union?

They are: Vermont, 1791; Kentucky, 1792; Tennessee, 1796; Ohio, 1802; Louisiana, 1812; Indiana, 1816; Mississippi, 1817; Illinois, 1818; Alabama, 1819; Maine, 1820; Missouri, 1821; Arkansas, 1836; Michigan, 1837; Florida, 1845; Iowa, 1845; Texas, 1845; Wisconsin, 1848; California, 1850; Minnesota, 1858; Oregon, 1859; Kansas, 1860; West Virginia, 1862; Nevada, 1864; Nebraska, 1867; and Colorado, 1876.

How soon may four others be admitted?

As soon as their constitutions are approved by Congress, as has been stated before.

Name some of those States that were formed out of parts of States already organized?

Vermont, out of New York; Maine, out of Massachusetts, and West Virginia, out of Virginia.

From what were most of the other new States formed?

From the Northwest Territory, acquired with independence in 1783; from the Louisiana Territory, purchased in 1803; and from the vast territory acquired in consequence of the Mexican War.

What is done with territory not belonging to any individual State, but to the United States?

It is governed under the direction of the United States Congress.

Is there any limitation to the power of Congress in this regard?

Yes; it can do nothing prejudicial to the claims of the United States or of any particular State.

Why was this restriction placed?

Because at the time when the Constitution was adopted some titles to land in the Western Territory were in dispute.

Repeat the clause referring to the Territories ?

" The Congress shall have power to dispose of, and make all needful rules and regulations respecting, the territory or other property belonging to the United States ; and nothing in this Constitution shall be so construed as to prejudice any claims of the United States, or of any particular State."

What are the Territories now belonging to the United States ?

They are, besides the District of Columbia, the various military and naval stations, and the former Territories now preparing for Statehood, the Territories of Utah, Wyoming, Idaho, New Mexico, Arizona, and the Indian Territory.

What former Territories are now preparing for Statehood ?

Dakota (to form two States), Washington, and Montana.

How are the Territories governed ?

By a governor appointed by the President and a legislature elected by the citizens in each Territory.

Are they represented in Congress ?

Yes, by one member from each Territory.

What is peculiar about the members of Congress from the Territories ?

They can take part in debates, but not in divisions or votes of the House of Representatives.

Is there any franchise limitation peculiar to the Territories ?

Yes; the citizens cannot vote in Presidential elections.

Is a State at liberty to choose a form of government for itself?

No; it is limited to the republican form.

How is this done?

By the provision in Section 4 of Article IV., that "the United States shall guarantee to every State in this Union a republican form of government."

What else is the United States obliged to do for each State?

To protect it against invasion and domestic violence.

What is meant by domestic violence?

Riots and insurrections.

In such cases how is the assistance of the United States to be obtained?

By petition from the Legislature of the State, or, if the Legislature cannot be called together, by petition of the State Executive.

What are the words of the clause granting this protection?

> " The United States shall protect each of the States against invasion; and on application of the legislature, or of the executive (when the legislature cannot be convened), against domestic violence."

CHAPTER XXXVII.

HOW THE CONSTITUTION MAY BE AMENDED.

What is the subject of the fifth Article of the Constitution ?

The power of amending this fundamental law of the Union.

Why was such a provision made ?

Because the fathers of our country knew that the Constitution was only an experiment, and foresaw that what would suit their times might not be exactly suitable to future generations.

Did they make the power of amendment easy ?

No, they wisely hedged it around with serious difficulties.

Why was this a wise course ?

Because it kept the Constitution from being tampered with unless there was an almost universal demand for a change.

Has it been very much changed ?

No ; nearly all the amendments are in the nature of additions or explanations.

Have any changes been made ?

Yes, principally in two respects.

What are these ?

The method of electing the President and Vice-President, and the abolition of slavery, and consequent change of the method of assessment and apportionment in the former slave States.

What is requisite for the adoption of an amendment to the Constitution ?

The vote of two-thirds of both Houses of Congress,

or of the legislatures of two-thirds of the States, as
the first step ; and, as the second and last step, ratification by the legislatures or special conventions of
three-fourths of the States, as the Congress may
direct.

*Who, then, in the first instance, may propose amend-
ments to the Constitution ?*

The Congress, by a vote of two-thirds of both
Houses.

How besides may an amendment be proposed ?

By the votes of two-thirds of the legislatures of the
several States.

Repeat the words to this effect.

" The Congress, whenever two-thirds of both
Houses shall deem it necessary, shall propose
amendments to this Constitution ; or on the
application of the legislatures of two-thirds
of the several States."

What is the next step to be taken ?

Congress shall then call a convention.

What is this Convention called ?

A Constitutional Convention.

What is its duty ?

To propose amendments.

What is then done ?

The proposed amendments are submitted to the
States.

How do the States act on them ?

Either through their legislatures or through special
conventions called together for the purpose.

*When does a proposed amendment become a part of
the Constitution ?*

When it is adopted by three-fourths of the States
acting as stated above,

What are the words of the Constitution on this subject ?

" The Congress shall call a convention for proposing amendments, which shall be valid to all intents and purposes as part of this Constitution, when ratified by the legislatures of three-fourths of the several States, or by conventions in three-fourths thereof, as the one or the other mode of ratification may be proposed by the Congress."

Were any restrictions placed on the matter of amendment ?

Yes, formerly two exemptions were made, but now there is only one.

What has become of the other ?

It disappeared with the lapse of time.

What was that restriction ?

No amendment affecting the first and fourth clauses of the ninth section of the first article could be proposed before the year 1808.

What did these two clauses have reference to ?

The subject of slavery.

And what has become of slavery ?

It has been amended out of existence in the United States.

Repeat the words bearing on this protection to slavery.

" No amendment which may be made prior to the year one thousand eight hundred and eight shall in any manner affect the first and fourth clauses in the ninth section of the first article."

What is the subject still excluded from amendment ?

The representation of the States in the United States Senate.

Cannot this representation be changed at all ?
Not without the consent of the State.
What are the words to this effect ?
    " No State, without its consent, shall be de-
        prived of its equal suffrage in the Senate."
*How many amendments to the Constitution have been
adopted ?*
Fifteen.
When were they adopted ?
At various times between the years 1789 and
1870.
*What amendments were adopted by the First Con-
gress ?*
The first ten.
What is their character ?
They are in the nature of a **supplementary** bill of
rights.
When was the eleventh adopted ?
By the Third Congress.
To what does it refer ?
To restriction of the judicial power, as we have al-
ready seen in considering this subject.
What was the occasion of the Twelfth Amendment ?
The cumbrous and inconvenient working of the
original method of electing the President and Vice-
President.
And when was the original law changed ?
By the Eighth Congress, as we have seen already.
What occasioned the other three amendments ?
The civil war and the abolition of slavery.
*Can changes in the form of government give release
from obligations on account of the national debt ?*
No; the nation always remains responsible for its
debts.

How is this matter regulated ?
By the law of nations.
Was it necessary, then, to provide for it in the Constitution ?
No.
Was such a provision made, nevertheless ?
Yes, in the first clause of Article VI.
What does this clause say ?
> " All debts contracted, and engagements en-
> tered into, before the adoption of this Consti-
> tution shall be as valid against the United
> States under this Constitution as under the
> Confederation."

CHAPTER XXXVIII.

CHARACTER, SCOPE, AND RATIFICATION OF THE CONSTITUTION.

What is the character of the Constitution?
It is declared to be the supreme law of the land.
Where is this declaration made ?
In the second clause of Article VI.
What is there stated to be of equal power with it ?
The law made in conformity therewith.
What else ?
All treaties made under the authority of the United States.
Repeat the words bearing on this point.
> " This Constitution and the laws of the United
> States which shall be made in pursuance
> thereof; and all treaties made, or which

shall be made, under the authority of the United States, shall be the supreme law of the land."

Under what obligation do State judges lie in this regard?

They are bound thereby.

Can a State oppose no bar to this power?

No; here the State is powerless.

What are the words?

"And the judges in every State shall be bound thereby; anything in the constitution or laws of any State to the contrary notwithstanding."

Is an oath of office required of those serving under the Constitution?

Yes, of certain high officials.

Besides the President and Vice-President, of whom we have spoken already, who are required to take this oath?

Senators and Representatives in Congress, the members of the several State legislatures, and all executive and judicial officers, both of the United States and of the several States.

What form of oath are they not obliged to take?

That requiring a religious test.

Would it be unconstitutional to ask an official to take such an oath?

It would.

Why was this a remarkable provision?

Because it was an innovation in English-speaking countries.

Who were generally meant to be excluded by the religious test oaths?

Catholics, who had reason, therefore, to take pride in the Constitution of the United States.

Have they held office under it ?
Yes, Catholics have held almost every office, except those of President and Vice-President, from the Chief-Justiceship of the Supreme Court down.
Repeat the words forbidding the religious test.
  " No religious test shall ever be required as a qualification to any office or public trust under the United States."
When was the Constitution to go into effect ?
As soon as it was ratified by nine States.
When did this happen ?
Early in September, 1788.
Which was the ninth State ?
New Hampshire.
Was it binding on those that did not ratify ?
No, only on those that had ratified.
What two important commonwealths. soon followed New Hampshire ?
New York and Virginia, making eleven within the year.
What two were yet left ?
Rhode Island and North Carolina, which did not ratify until after the First Congress had met.
· Repeat the seventh Article, regulating the ratification of the Constitution.
  " The ratification of the conventions of nine States shall be sufficient for the establishment of this Constitution between the States so ratifying the same."
When was this ratification acted upon by Congress ?
On September 13, ˙1788, when eleven States, as we have seen, had given their assent.
What were these States ?
New Hampshire, Massachusetts, Connecticut, New

York, New Jersey, Pennsylvania, Delaware, Virginia, Maryland, South Carolina, and Georgia.

Had official notice been received from all these eleven States on September 13 ?

No; Delaware and Maryland had not yet been heard from.

In consequence of this ratification, what steps were taken by Congress ?

They first ordered that the States that had adopted the Constitution should name Presidential electors on the first Wednesday of the following January.

And what next ?

That on the first Wednesday of February following the electors should assemble in their several States and vote for a President.

And who was chosen President on this occasion ?

George Washington, by a unanimous vote.

And when were proceedings to begin under the new Congress ?

On the first Wednesday of March, 1789.

When was General Washington inducted into the office of the Presidency?

On April 30, 1789.

And where did this event take place?

In the city of New York.

How soon were amendments to the Constitution proposed ?   .

In the very first session of the First Congress; namely, in 1789.

Where was this session held, and when was it commenced ?

In New York, on March 4, 1789.

CHAPTER XXXIX.

RELIGIOUS LIBERTY.

What amendments were adopted by the First Congress?

The first ten of all that have been enacted so far.

What was their character?

They were in the nature of additions, and were simply a new declaration of rights.

With what subject does the first of these amendments deal?

With restrictions on the power of Congress.

What are the subjects of these restrictions?

Religious liberty, freedom of speech, and the right of assembly and petition for redress of grievances.

Repeat the words of the First Amendment.

"Congress shall make no law respecting an establishment of religion, or prohibiting the free exercise thereof; or abridging the freedom of speech or of the press; or the right of the people peaceably to assemble and to petition the Government for a redress of grievances."

What is peculiar about the "religious liberty" part of this article?

That it had its origin in religious intolerance.

How was this?

It was proposed on behalf of New Hampshire, which did not want its religious condition at that time to be interfered with.

How does this State stand in religious matters?

As the most intolerant in the Union.

How do you show this ?

By the fact that down to our own time it has refused to allow Catholics to hold office on account of their religion.

And what has been the result of the amendment as regards Catholics ?

They have been benefited by it throughout the entire country, and even the State most intolerant of them cannot much longer refuse them full liberty.

What other instance in the history of our country has shown an anti-Catholic movement to result for the benefit of Catholics ?

The Revolution itself, which was stimulated by anger on account of the Quebec Act.

What are the restrictions on Congress in regard to religion ?

First, that it shall make no law establishing any denomination as the religion of the State; and second, that it shall not by law prohibit the free exercise of any form of Christianity.

Why do you say " Christianity" ?

Because it has been decided by the Supreme Court that Christianity is a fundamental part of our Constitution.

CHAPTER XL.

FREEDOM OF THE PRESS AND OF THE PERSON.

• What is the position of the press under our Constitution ?
It is absolutely free to discuss all public questions.
And what public and political rights have the people ?
All that are consistent with the public peace.
What may the people do towards redressing their wrongs ?
They may assemble peaceably and present petitions to the Government demanding a redress of grievances.
To what does the Second Amendment refer ?
To the right of the people to keep and bear arms.
Why is this right not infringed ?
Because a well-regulated militia is necessary to the security of a free State.
What are the words of this amendment ?
" A well-regulated militia being necessary to the security of a free state, the right of the people to keep and bear arms shall not be infringed."
What is the subject of the Third Amendment ?
The quartering of soldiers, both in time of peace and in time of war.
Why was this provision thought of ?
Because of the custom that had prevailed everywhere of billeting soldiers on private citizens and thereby causing great annoyance.

Repeat the words of this article.

"No soldier shall, in time of peace, be quartered in any house without the consent of the owner; nor in time of war but in a manner to be prescribed by law."

What protection is guaranteed to the citizens by the Fourth Amendment?

The right to be secure in their persons, homes, and property without due warranty of law.

How far does this right extend?

To the protection of the citizen against arrest or annoyance unless sufficient cause can be shown for troubling him.

And even when this is produced, what protection has he?

That of the *habeas corpus* act, by which his case can be investigated at once.

Repeat the Fourth Article of the amendments.

"The right of the people to be secure in their persons, houses, papers, and effects against unreasonable searches and seizures shall not be violated; and no warrant shall issue but upon probable cause, supported by oath or affirmation, and particularly describing the place to be searched and the persons or things to be seized."

CHAPTER XLI.

PRIVILEGES OF ACCUSED PERSONS.

What is the subject of the next article ?
The proceedings against persons charged with crimes, and the rights of such persons.

What is necessary to the holding of a person on a charge of having committed an infamous crime ?
Generally an indictment by a grand jury.

Why do you say "generally" ?
Because a special rule applies to cases arising in the army or the militia when in actual service.

What are the words bearing on the jury indictment ?
" No person shall be held to answer for a capital or otherwise infamous crime, unless on a presentment or indictment of a grand jury."

How are the exceptions to this rule specified ?
" Except in cases arising in the land or naval forces, or in the militia, when in actual service, in time of war or public danger."

How are these cases tried ?
By court-martial.

If a person is once acquitted of a crime, can he or she be tried again for the same ?
No.

Why is this ?
Because of a provision in the Fifth Amendment forbidding it.

What is this provision ?
" Nor shall any person be subject for the same offence to be twice put in jeopardy of life or limb."

But can a person once convicted be tried again for the same offence ?

Yes ; in nearly all cases a new trial can be had for reasonable cause.

May a person be a witness against himself ?

Not without his or her consent.

How is this provided for ?

Nor shall any person, it is said in the Fifth Amendment, " be compelled, in any criminal case, to be a witness against himself."

What further guarantees are, then, secured to the citizen ?

He shall not " be deprived of life, liberty, or property without due process of law."

How is the right of private property guaranteed ?

Full compensation must be made for all of it taken for public use.

Repeat the words to this effect.

" Nor shall private property be taken for public use without just compensation."

Are any other rights guaranteed ?

Yes, several.

Name one of them.

That of an accused person to a speedy and public trial.

How shall this trial be conducted ?

By an impartial jury.

From among whom must the members of this jury be taken ?

From among the inhabitants of the district in which the crime has been committed.

How is this district determined ?

It must have been previously ascertained by law.

What are the words making these regulations ?
Those of the first part of the Sixth Amendment, namely:

"In all criminal prosecutions the accused shall enjoy the right to a speedy and public trial, by an impartial jury of the State and district wherein the crime shall have been committed, which district shall have been previously ascertained by law."

What is the next right guaranteed to the accused ?
That he "be informed of the nature and cause of the accusation."

Has he any rights as to witnesses ?
Yes; both as to those for and those against him.

What right has he with regard to witnesses against him ?
He can demand to be confronted with them.

And as to those in his favor ?
He may call for compulsory process for obtaining such.

Repeat the words in reference to witnesses.

"The accused shall enjoy the right to be confronted with the witnesses against him; to have compulsory process for obtaining witnesses in his favor."

What other right has the accused ?
"To have the assistance of counsel for his defence."

Does the right of trial by jury apply to civil as well as to criminal cases ?
Yes, unless where the value in controversy is less than twenty dollars.

Where is this provision laid down ?
In the Seventh Amendment.

What are the words here as to the right of trial by jury?

> "In suits at common law, where the value in controversy shall exceed twenty dollars, the right of trial by jury shall be preserved."

How is a jury trial to be conducted?

According to the rules of the Common Law.

How is this regulated?

By the concluding words of Article VII. of the amendments.

What are they?

> "And no fact tried by a jury shall be otherwise re-examined in any court of the United States than according to the rules of the common law."

What is the subject of the Eighth Article?

Bail, fines, and punishments.

What is said of them?

That they must not be excessive.

Repeat the words.

> "Excessive bail shall not be required, nor excessive fines imposed, nor cruel and unusual punishments inflicted."

Does the Constitution contain a complete enumeration of rights?

No; this would be practically impossible.

And what of those not enumerated?

They are not disparaged by this enumeration.

Are they retained by the people?

Such of them are as originally belonged to the people.

Where is this provision made as to this construction of the Constitution?

In the Ninth Amendment.

What does it say?

" The enumeration in the Constitution of certain rights shall not be construed to deny or disparage others retained by the people."

What is the subject of the Tenth amendment?

Powers reserved to the States.

What is there said of these powers?

" The powers not delegated to the United States by the Constitution, nor prohibited by it to the States, are reserved to the States respectively, or to the people."

When were the next two amendments adopted?

The Eleventh at the second session of the Third Congress, and the Twelfth at the first session of the Eighth Congress.

Of what subjects respectively do they treat?

The former of the restriction of judicial powers, and the latter of the mode of electing the President and Vice-President of the United States.

Why is it not necessary to dwell upon these two amendments here?

Because they have been discussed already in treating of the Judiciary and the Presidency.

CHAPTER XLII.

THE ABOLITION OF SLAVERY.

How much time elapsed before another amendment to the Constitution was adopted ?

Over sixty years.

What occasioned the adoption of the Thirteenth Amendment ?

The changed condition of the negro race in the United States that resulted from our civil war.

What is the subject of this amendment ?

The abolition of slavery in the United States.

How and when was slavery abolished here ?

By proclamation of President Lincoln in 1863.

What, then, was the necessity for the amendment ?

To give full legal sanction to the President's act.

Was this result one in which Catholics should rejoice?

Yes, because the Church has ever striven in the same direction, either doing away with slavery altogether where she could, or trying to mitigate its severities where she could not abolish it.

Has all involuntary servitude been totally abolished in our country ?

No; it still remains for the punishment of convicted criminals.

Repeat the Thirteenth Amendment.

" Neither slavery nor involuntary servitude, except as a punishment for crime, whereof the party shall have been duly convicted, shall exist within the United States or any place subject to their jurisdiction."

When was this amendment adopted ?
In 1865.

Did it confer the rights of citizenship and suffrage on the negroes who had been slaves ?
No; two further amendments had to be proposed for this purpose.

Were such adopted ?
Yes; one in 1868 and the other in 1870; and they are known as the Fourteenth and Fifteenth Amendments, the former treating of the right of citizenship, and the latter of the right of suffrage.

What declaration is made as to the right of citizenship ?

" All persons born or naturalized in the United
States, and subject to the jurisdiction thereof,
are citizens of the United States and of the
State wherein they reside."

May a State infringe upon the rights of citizenship ?
No; for it is declared in the same first section of the Fourteenth Amendment that

" No State shall make or enforce any law
which shall abridge the privileges or immu-
nities of citizens of the United States."

Are all the rights of legal procedure likewise guaranteed to all citizens ?
Yes; for it is said:

" Nor shall any State deprive any person of
life, liberty, or property without due process
of law, nor deny to any person within its
jurisdiction the equal protection of the laws."

Besides its bearing on the freed negroes, what is important about the second section of the Fourteenth Amendment ?
It modifies the third clause of the second section of Article I. of the Constitution.

In what respect ?

In respect to the mode of enumerating the popu‑
lation for the purpose of the representation of the
State in Congress.

What was the old way ?

In the slave States there was representation only
for three-fifths of the number of slaves.

And what change was made ?

It was ordered that

"Representatives shall be apportioned among
the several States according to their respect‑
ive numbers, counting the whole number of
persons in each State, excluding Indians not
taxed."

*Besides these Indians, were any others deducted from
the population for purposes of representation ?*

Yes; when any male inhabitants of such State, of
twenty-one years or over, who were citizens of the
United States, were deprived of the franchise, except
for participation in rebellion or crime, then the State
was deprived of representation in the proportion
which such disfranchised citizens have to the entire
population of the State.

What was the meaning of this restriction ?

Abridging the representation in Congress of those
States that might refuse the electoral franchise to the
freed negroes.

How long did this restriction remain in force ?

Until the adoption of the Fifteenth Amendment,
extending to all such persons the right of suffrage.

Repeat this restrictive provision.

"But when the right to vote at any election
for the choice of electors for President and
Vice-President of the United States, repre-

sentatives in Congress, the executive and judicial officers of a State, or the members of the legislature thereof, is denied to any of the male inhabitants of such State, being twenty-one years of age and citizens of the United States, or in any way abridged, except for participation in rebellion or other crime, the basis of representation therein shall be reduced in the proportion which such male citizens shall bear to the whole number of male citizens twenty-one years of age in such State."

To what does the third section of the Fourteenth Amendment refer ?

To the excluding of certain persons from holding office under the United States.

Who are so excluded ?

All former office-holders who, having taken the oath of office under the United States, have engaged in rebellion against the Union.

Are they for ever and irretrievably debarred from such office-holding ?

No ; Congress may remove the disability.

How ?

By a two-thirds vote of each House.

Repeat this section.

" No person shall be a Senator or Representative in Congress, or elector of President and Vice-President, or hold any office, civil or military, under the United States or under any State, who, having previously taken an oath as a member of Congress, or as an officer of the United States, or as a member of any State Legislature, or as an executive

or judicial officer of any State, to support the
Constitution of the United States, shall have
engaged in insurrection or rebellion against
the same, or given aid or comfort to the
enemies thereof. But Congress may, by a
vote of two-thirds of each House, remove
such disability."

What other provision is made by this amendment ? .

The establishing of the validity of debts incurred
by the Federal Government in suppressing rebellion
and the repudiation of all debts and claims contracted
or made by those who may have lost by taking part
in rebellion.

*What are the words of the section making this pro-
vision ?*

" The validity of the public debt of the United
States, authorized by law, including debts
incurred for payment of pensions and boun-
ties for services in suppressing insurrection
and rebellion, shall not be questioned. But
neither the United States nor any State shall
assume or pay any debt or obligation incurred in aid of insurrection or rebellion
against the United States, or any claim for
the loss or emancipation of any slave, but
all such debts, obligations, and claims shall
be held illegal and void."

*By what provision was the right of suffrage extended
to those who had formerly been slaves ?*

By the Fifteenth Amendment.

How does it read ?

Thus :

" The right of citizens of the United States to
vote shall not be denied or abridged by the

United States, or by any State, on account
of race, color, or previous condition of servitude."

What is peculiar about the last three amendments ?
Each has what is called an enacting clause.

What is its purport ?
That Congress shall have power to enforce each
article by appropriate legislation.

CHAPTER XLIII.

STATE GOVERNMENT.

*Is the Constitution of the United States purely and
simply an original instrument ?*
No; it was derived in large part from the State
constitutions.

And what was the origin of these latter ?
The royal grants, patents, and charters by virtue of
which the British colonies in America were established.

*Did the States, in forming the Federal Constitution,
surrender all functions of government to the central
authority ?*
No; on the contrary, whatever powers are not
therein mentioned were retained by the States.

How far do these powers extend ?
To the administration of all public affairs within
the limits of the State, in such a way as does not
conflict with the United States Constitution, and even
to punishment for treason against the State.

How is this administration carried on ?

By a triple system of government like that of the United States, having legislative, judiciary, and executive departments.

Does the central government retain any control of the State governments ?

Only as to the form of these governments and the protection of citizens of the United States provided for by the Fourteenth and Fifteenth Amendments to the Constitution.

What must the form of the State government be ?

The republican form.

How are new States added to the Union ?

By the division of States already organized or out of communities occupying territory belonging to the United States.

When may such a territory be changed into a State ?

When it has a population capable of self-government equal to at least that of a Congressional district according to the preceding United States census.

What is the first step towards Statehood ?

The passing by Congress of an " enabling act."

What is authorized by this act ?

The holding of a convention of delegates elected by the male citizens of the Territory for the purpose of drafting and adopting a State constitution.

Does this constitution become operative as soon as it is adopted ?

No; it must be submitted to the United States Congress for approval.

What is the next step ?

If the proposed constitution is approved by Congress, a new State is declared added to the Union, and on the next ensuing fourth day of July another star appears on the United States flag.

What was the last State thus admitted ?
· Colorado, in 1876.

Are any others now preparing for admission ?
Yes, four; namely, North Dakota, South Dakota, Montana, and Washington, in whose favor the Enabling Act was signed by President Cleveland on February 22, 1889.

What, then, is a State constitution ?
It is " a comprehensive fundamental law, or, rather, group of laws included in one instrument, which has been directly enacted by the people of the State."

Must this law remain permanently unchanged ?
No ; it may be repealed or altered.

By whom ?
By the people of the State themselves, and not merely by their representatives.

Who are the chief instruments of a State organization ?
A Governor and certain other officials elected for a short term of years, a legislature of two branches similarly elected, and a judiciary chosen for a long term of years.

What are the functions of a Governor ?
For his State they are similar to those of the President for the United States.

And of the other State officers ?
Duties corresponding to those of the President's Cabinet.

Is there a State officer corresponding to the Vice-President of the United States ?
Yes ; the Lieutenant-Governor.

What are his duties ?
To take the Governor's place during the absence or inability of the latter, and to preside over the deliberations of the State Senate.

Are the Governor and other State officers chosen for the same length of time in all the States ?

No; in some States they are elected only for one year, in some for two, in some for three, and in some for four years.

Are they always eligible for re-election ?

No; or at least not for consecutive terms, as in Pennsylvania, for instance.

How are they chosen ?

By the direct vote of the people generally, but not always.

When does the exception arise ?

When a candidate fails to receive a clear majority of all the votes cast, as is the law in some of the New England States.

In such case how is choice made ?

By the State Legislature, both branches voting together.

May the Governor be punished for improperly administering his office ?

Yes; he may be impeached by the lower branch of the Legislature and tried by the State Senate.

Were State Legislatures always composed of two branches ?

No; originally some States, like Pennsylvania and Georgia, had only one legislative chamber.

Why was a change made in these cases ?

Because it was found necessary to place a check on an assembly too apt to be controlled by popular passion.

What is the difference between the two branches of the Legislature ?

The Senate has a much smaller membership than the lower branch.

How does this happen ?

By a Senator representing a far larger constituency than does a member of the Assembly, or House of Representatives, or House of Delegates, etc., as the lower branch is variously called in different States.

Is there any difference in the mode of election ?

No ; they are both chosen by popular vote.

What is their function ?

To enact laws bearing on State matters, just as Congress does for the United States.

Are their enactments subject to any control ?

Yes ; the Governor has the *veto* power as has the President, and in the same manner must be over-ruled by a two-thirds vote of both Houses before the bill can become a law.

Are the Senators and Representatives elected for the same length of term ?

No ; the term of the former is usually twice as long as that of the latter.

What of the State judiciary ?

It is constituted in a graded manner, like that of the Federal system.

Are the various grades known by the same name in the different States ?

Generally they are, but not always.

By what name is the highest State court usually designated ?

As the Supreme Court ; but in some instances it is otherwise, as in New York State, where it is called the Court of Appeals.

Has New York no tribunal known as the Supreme Court ?

Yes, but it is really only a Circuit Court.

What are the lowest judicial functions ?

In cities, those of police and civil justices, as in New York, and those of magistrates, as in Philadelphia ; and in rural districts, those of squires and burgesses.

Do they go by these names everywhere ?

No ; they have various names in different States.

What are the courts of ordinary jurisdiction called ?

The Courts of Common Pleas.

Have we separate equity courts ?

Not generally, the Common Pleas having been entrusted with equity jurisdiction in most cases.

What State presents an exception to the ordinary arrangement of the Courts ?

New Jersey, which adheres most strictly to the ancient forms, and whose system requires special study.

How far does the jurisdiction of the State courts extend ?

To all cases except those to which a State or the United States is a party.

When, then, may an appeal be made from a State to a Federal Court ?

Only in cases touching Federal legislation or the Federal Constitution.

What is the relation of the State in regard to the question of taxation of its citizens ?

It may levy such taxes, under authority of proper legislation, as are necessary for the support of its government.

May it delegate this authority ?

Yes, and it does actually delegate it to properly constituted local bodies in cities, counties, townships, and school districts.

In what form are State and local taxes levied ?

In the form of direct taxation, according to a systematic assessment of real and personal property.

CHAPTER XLIV.

CITY GOVERNMENT.

What is the most important of the local governments subordinate to the State ?

That of cities.

After what model is a city government usually formed ?

After the State and the Federal Government.

Whence does city government derive its authority ?

From the State.

What is usually the name of the instrument granting this authority ?

A charter.

May a charter be revised or revoked ?

It may, and the city may lawfully be left without any local government.

Who would rule it in this case ?

The State authorities or persons delegated by them.

By what name is the chief official in a city called ?

The Mayor.

How is he chosen ?

By direct popular vote.

Does he govern the city alone ?

No; he is aided by other officials, either elected like himself, or appointed by him, and by a representative body of men representing districts of the city.

What is this body called ?

City Councils, or a Board of Aldermen.

Is this body constituted alike in every city ?

No; in some cities, as in New York, it consists of only one chamber, while in others, like Philadelphia, it has two.

What is its duty ?

To legislate on purely local affairs.

Without control ?

No; subject to the Mayor's veto power, which is regulated like that of the Governor or the President.

How do our city governments compare with those of the State and the Federal authority ?

Not favorably, as they have always been more subject to corrupt influences.

How do you account for this ?

By the fact that in cities there are more men of leisure who make a profession of politics and turn the offices to account for their own emolument.

How may this evil be corrected ?

By enacting and enforcing severe penalties for all breaches of public trust.

With this reserve, what conclusion should we arrive at regarding our thoroughly localized system of Government ?

That it is the best guarantee of civic freedom, it being extremely difficult to administer "a vast territory and population from one centre and by one government."

www.ingramcontent.com/pod-product-compliance
Lightning Source LLC
Chambersburg PA
CBHW031548260326
41914CB00002B/319